Creative Aging

Rethinking Retirement and Non-Retirement in a Changing World

Marjory Zoet Bankson

Walking Together, Finding the Way®
SKYLIGHT PATHS®
PUBLISHING
Woodstock, Vermont

Creative Aging: Rethinking Retirement and Non-Retirement in a Changing World

2011 Quality Paperback Edition, Third Printing
© 2010 by Marjory Zoet Bankson

Scripture quotations are from the *New Revised Standard Version Bible,* copyright © 1989 by the Division of Christian Education of the National Council of the Churches of Christ in the USA. Used by permission. All rights reserved.

The stories shared in this book are true, but the names of most people have been changed to protect the privacy of each individual.

Library of Congress Cataloging-in-Publication Data
Bankson, Marjory Zoet.
  Creative aging : rethinking retirement and non-retirement in a changing world / Marjory Zoet Bankson.—2010 quality paperback ed.
      p. cm.
  Includes bibliographical references.
  ISBN-13: 978-1-59473-281-2 (quality pbk.)
  ISBN-10: 1-59473-281-7 (quality pbk.)
  1. Retirement. 2. Retirement—Psychological aspects. 3. Retirees—Conduct of life. 4. Self-actualization (Psychology) 5. Aging. I. Title.

                                                                    HQ1062.B36 2010
  248.8'5—dc22

10 9 8 7 6 5 4 3
Manufactured in the United States of America
Cover design: Tim Holtz
Cover photo: © Robert Findlay. Image from BigStockPhoto.com.

SkyLight Paths Publishing is creating a place where people of different spiritual traditions come together for challenge and inspiration, a place where we can help each other understand the mystery that lies at the heart of our existence.

SkyLight Paths sees both believers and seekers as a community that increasingly transcends traditional boundaries of religion and denomination—people wanting to learn from each other, *walking together, finding the way.*

SkyLight Paths, "Walking Together, Finding the Way," and colophon are trademarks of LongHill Partners, Inc., registered in the U.S. Patent and Trademark Office.

Walking Together, Finding the Way®
Published by SkyLight Paths Publishing
A Division of Longhill Partners, Inc.
Sunset Farm Offices, Route 4, P.O. Box 237
Woodstock, VT 05091
Tel: (802) 457-4000   Fax: (802) 457-4004
www.skylightpaths.com

For my mother, Edna McLaurin Zoet,
who found her true self late in life.

Contents

Acknowledgments

To all those who shared their stories with me about this amazing new period of generativity: As we've explored what it means to age at this time in history, I have tried to tend your stories with respect and care, giving you some privacy by changing names, but otherwise keeping the details straight. Together we are coming to a new level of consciousness about why we are here, now.

To the members of Seekers Church, who have been my extended family while I struggled to find my encore work: You have walked with me, challenged me, and celebrated important passages along the way. As I became more conscious of the third round of call, beyond identity and vocation, you encouraged me to write it down and pass it on.

To my husband, Peter, for his patience and understanding of my call to write. You helped keep the household rhythms of meals and conversation from disappearing altogether. You guarded those Sabbath times that make this work a joy instead of bondage, and you kept my spirits up when I could not see the way forward.

And to Marcia, my editor and friend, who has once again helped me make sense of the circular style of my writing. Without you, this book would not have been born.

INTRODUCTION
Making the Extra Years Count

On my sixtieth birthday, I stood in a small circle of women who were older than I. Shadows stretched across the dry grass, and an evening breeze sent a few dry leaves around my feet. We had spent the day together on retreat, and this was our final ritual. Starting from a large circle that included women of many different ages, we had moved inward by decades, naming the primary markers of each time span, and then leaving behind those who had not yet passed the next decade birthday.

From their own experiences, the women in the over-sixty circle told me that the decade ahead would probably hold three things: the end of my career, coping with a major health crisis for me or my spouse, and the necessity for sending down deeper spiritual roots to deal with the diminishments of aging. They blessed me with their close warm bodies and their prayers and urged me to celebrate the good in each day and each decade.

As I look back to that circle of women, I'm struck by the fact that they did not identify the new wellsprings of creative work that have bubbled up since my sixtieth birthday. Perhaps they were simply speaking out of their own experience. Perhaps they were hardly aware of the new beginnings they were experiencing themselves.

In truth, the generative period between the ages of (roughly) sixty and seventy-five is a period of possibility that is almost new in our time. When Social Security was inaugurated during the New Deal, actuarial tables predicted death soon after the age of sixty-five. Today, women can expect to live beyond eighty and men, just a few years less. This extended life span presents us with the need to grapple with the question, "What is this period for?"

With more education and better health care available after World War II, women entered the workplace in large numbers during the 1980s and '90s. They juggled family and work commitments and demonstrated a remarkable entrepreneurial spirit. Today, women-owned businesses employ twenty-three million people, nearly double the fifty largest companies combined. Men have grown up with more expectation that they will share family and work responsibilities more equally with women. Now, as the early boomers reach traditional retirement age, both men and women are wanting to work in new areas, to be useful without feeling used or taken for granted.

Beyond our adult work or career stretches a span of ten or fifteen years in which most of us have valuable experience to offer but very little cultural expectation of being productive. Some might continue in their old career track, like some of the elder statesmen newscasters on television. Others, as pictured in *AARP The Magazine*, will focus on exercising to stay fit and traveling to stay intellectually engaged. Still, others will become easy targets for unrelenting ads for leisure living: endless activity, a gated community, and help when health fails. Much in our culture sends the message that endless leisure is the reward for our striving, and there are countless articles about stretching our financial resources to cover these "golden years." However, there is a great shortage of discussion about the inner work of making our aging years creative and meaningful. That's what I want to explore in this book.

I think it's an incredible gift to be alive at this time in history. Never before have so many Americans reached retirement age with a social consciousness, advanced education, and such good health. Never before have so many women arrived at this milestone with so much experience with organizing others for a common purpose, or men who have been sensitized to the needs of children through more participation in family life. It is also clear that this boomer wave of our population has largely avoided traditional religious structures and sought spiritual guidance from many sources, so the practice of giving to others, of service to the community, is more personal and less institutional than in earlier times.

Financial need is obviously one reason for continuing to work, but our human need to feel useful and connected to the world around us is another major factor. The boomer age group has changed social structures of education, family, and work patterns as they have moved through each stage of life. Now they are changing the terrain of retirement with "encore" careers and a new global awareness. By the sheer force of their numbers, boomers will change the face of aging. And with the financial meltdown, there is even more impetus to change patterns, create new work, and explore part-time employment, as well as volunteer service.

Rather than the doom and gloom predictions that the boomer generation will bankrupt the nation with needs, I am hopeful that the activism that has characterized this age group will once again chart a new path. Right now, American society is not organized to welcome older workers who want to use their years of experience in a new way. Speed and efficiency seem to be the measure of the marketplace, but I am optimistic about the creative spirit that I see among people who are wanting to work with less pressure and more personal contact and move into a new field for a ten- to fifteen-year period after age sixty.

And surely part of my excitement is that this generative period is my story, too. What excites me about postcareer creativity is that it seems to arise from a deeper spiritual stratum—a layer of soul compressed under the pile of ego expectations and responsibilities that come from work and family needs in an earlier career stage.

I have been searching for an accurate way to describe the inner and outer dimensions of this generative period that we have been granted by less arduous labor and better health care. The word "retirement" doesn't seem appropriate anymore, except to describe a change of pace, completion of the all-consuming phase of full-time work that we typically undertake as adults. Marc Freedman, CEO and founder of Civic Ventures, in his book *Prime Time*, describes this postcareer period as the "encore years." Author and journalist Abigail Trafford calls it a "bonus decade" in her book *My Time*. Sociologist Sara Lawrence-Lightfoot calls it the "third chapter" in her book *The Third*

Chapter: Passion, Risk, and Adventure in the 25 Years After 50. Clearly, we are rethinking retirement and non-retirement in a changing world.

As I listened to people describe their hopes and dreams for this extra period of productive energy, I heard their creativity emerging, as well as what I term their "call"—a calling to find purpose and act in the world. Instead of buying a lifestyle of leisure and putting in time until we die, I discovered people who were actively engaged in community service and spiritual discovery. They wanted to work, but not quite so hard or long. They believed in longer life with a purpose. Most wanted to make a difference with the extra time they had been granted. Our task is to discover what our call is at this age and stage of life and to invent new ways to live that out.

Every time we come to a major transition in our lives, there is a predictable pattern to our response to change and the ambivalence of an unknown future. Although we may not move through the pattern of transition in exactly the order described below, these steps encompass the issues that will need to be addressed if we want to make a successful transition from a professional career to generativity in our encore years.

It is especially important, when we leave the primary occupation that has given us position and a paycheck, to attend to the inner work of grief and loss before we get to a new beginning. Chapters 2 through 8 explore the seven phases of transition, beginning with letting go:

- Release: letting go of the vocational identity associated with our career or primary work.
- Resistance: feeling stuck, stagnant, resistant to change.
- Reclaiming: drawing energy from the past, discovering unused gifts.
- Revelation: forming or finding a new vision of the future.
- Crossing point: moving from stagnation to generativity.
- Risk: stepping out into the world with a new vision.
- Relating: finding or creating new structures for a new kind of work.

Although this book is not a scientific or systematic study, I did interview men and women in various regions of the country who were interested in doing something different with this generative period of their lives. Most had a college education and professional experience and had enough financial security to take some time with this transition, although nearly all wanted to work for some income.

I used a "snowball method" of investigation, interviewing other people recommended by my initial subjects. Many said they wanted to move from being responsible for an entire department or program to short-term projects. They wanted to feel useful without feeling "used." Instead of buying into retirement as years of endless golf games, these people talked about wanting to use their time to give forward, to notice needs in their community (however small or large) and find a place where they could continue to learn, grow, and serve a greater good. It was their desire to continue growing and learning that led to the title *Creative Aging: Rethinking Retirement and Non-Retirement in a Changing World.*

If you are approaching this important transition stage, or know somebody who is, I hope you will give yourself the time to ponder the questions at the end of each chapter and try the spiritual practices that I have suggested for each step in this round of call. We cannot do this important work alone. You may want to find others who will share the journey with you.

I firmly believe that there is a reason why we are alive at this time in history, with our education and experience. We have an unprecedented opportunity to grow, learn, and offer our unique gifts to the world. Out of the darkness, dawn comes. Let's make these extra years count.

1

WHAT NOW?

Rethinking Aging

Listen to your life. See it for the fathomless mystery
that it is. In the boredom and pain of it no less than in
the excitement and gladness: touch, taste, smell your
way to the holy and hidden heart of it.

—Frederick Buechner, *Now and Then*

As we approach midlife, many of us begin to think about what
will make our lives worth living in our sixties and seventies.
Most of us do not feel particularly old or worn-out, and yet we are
looking for ways to slow down and notice things we have been too
busy to consider before. We may begin looking for a place where
we do not have to compete so fiercely or carry the ambitions of
others in quite the same way.

The question of "What now?" sharpens as we leave a challenging
career and realize that we probably have ten or fifteen productive
years ahead of us. Although hobbies and volunteer work do provide
a creative outlet for many people as they age, I think there is a more
important aspect of creative aging that takes us to the interior geography of finding new purpose, a new call, in our later years. Many
people focus on being with grandchildren, but that is surely not
enough (unless it means becoming a full-time parent). Others return
to earlier enjoyments, only to find that physical limits have set in
since the last time they biked any distance or sang with a chorus.

For me, the notion of call is the inner nudge to wake up and notice our place in the greater scheme of things. I see call not as a strictly vocational choice, but as a special way of understanding what we are here for, our reason for being. Finding my call has been a guiding impulse since my teenage years when I used to practice the pipe organ in a mortuary, sharing the space with whoever had died that week. I began to realize that whatever made that person alive was now gone and would never return. That aliveness was in me, too, and I wondered why I was here. Was there a divine pattern in creation? Did I have a part in it? Where did my soul come from? And where did it go? What was my purpose?

The Spiral of Call

The story of Moses and the burning bush gave me language for some of the questions I was asking as a teenager—and many of us face again as we age. As an outlaw, far from home, Moses was startled to see a burning bush and hear a voice saying to him, "Take off your shoes. You are standing on holy ground" (Exodus 3:5). The call to recognize that he was already standing on the holy ground of his own life began a relationship with God that had many different chapters. As Moses grew in his understanding of that mysterious presence in the burning bush, it seemed to open him to a journey of being continually called to awareness, of waking up to the spiritual dimensions at each new stage of his life.

The first round of Moses's call was to discover his place in God's story, his identity. He needed to know whether he was an orphaned slave, a prince of Egypt, an escaped killer with hallucinations, or something more—one who was being called to lead his people out of Egypt.

Once he was successful in that first task, after he had led his people across the Red Sea, and they began their wilderness wandering, Moses settled into his identity as a leader and focused on his work, which was to help his people link their desert experience with God's guidance. The second round of Moses's call was to understand his true vocation as a leader and to explore both its inner and outer dimensions.

Finally, the third round of Moses's call was to understand his gift of a unique relationship with God, separate from his role as a leader. He did not have the luxury of retirement. He needed to revisit the earlier questions of identity and reassure himself that he still had God's ear as he argued with God on behalf of his people. Even though he, like the rest of his generation, would not enter the Promised Land himself, he came to understand his unique role in the ongoing story of his people.

Moses's call, which began with the burning bush, seemed to spiral throughout his life, growing and changing with the different circumstances he faced. Each time a major crisis arose, he had to think and pray his way through the same questions: "Who am I to God? What am I being asked to do? Will the people accept my leadership?" The answers to those questions were never settled. It was not a linear progression from one stage to the next. Instead, Moses lived out a spiral pattern of call that kept revisiting those questions throughout his life.

Every time we face a new transition in our lives, we also begin a new round in the spiral of call. And each time, we revisit the same questions that Moses faced: "Who am I now? What is my work here?" And later, "What is my unique gift?" These are not stages to be accomplished or rungs to be climbed. I think of these stages more like rounds of a slinky toy, sometimes compact and solid, like rings stacked one on top of the other, and sometimes stretched out like an uncurled extension cord, each round separate from the next.

The spiral of call resounds throughout our lives, calling us to consciousness and creativity, again and again. Embracing the spiral of call means that we have something to look forward to, always. Too often, people narrow the concept of call to ordained ministry. I see it more broadly, as the inner voice that tells us that we are part of the ongoing creation story. Call invites us to wake up, to know our lives matter and our decisions make a difference to the vibrant network of life on this planet.

Is This All There Is?

A typical complaint in our fifties is to wonder, "Is this all there is?" As we approach age sixty, many people fall into stasis or a mild form of depression or, as psychologist Erik H. Erikson calls it, "stagnation." Erikson defined the tension of this period of adult development in his book *Childhood and Society,* calling the developmental task at this time of life "generativity versus stagnation." When we have explored the inner and outer dimensions of our primary career focus, it is not surprising that a kind of repetitive rigidity sets in, as though we have finished what we are here for and don't know what to do with the life energy that we still have.

I don't know anybody who really chooses stagnation, but it can happen if we have overidentified with external systems (role, title, paycheck, position) where we are no longer needed. We can get stuck in trying to repeat what we have done well in the past or simply sink into depression, feeling discarded, useless, and worthless. This threat is growing as technology makes the outsourcing of "knowledge work" more frequent, and organizations disappear into a sea of corporate mergers and buyouts. When meaning and purpose are defined as economic success, then job loss or being outmoded makes aging a threat to be feared or denied. Not only do individuals stagnate, but institutions do as well. Too many companies and institutions mandate retirement rather than shifting their organizational structures to retain elders who could offer much-needed wisdom and experience.

Since World War II, we have achieved a life span that allows more of us to do the inner work of conscious integration and wholeness, to recover the creativity we were born with and begin to apply it in new ways. As the boomer generation begins to retire, we have an unprecedented need for new ways to understand the purpose for aging. We have already learned what we do well. If anything, our skills have so defined us that even success becomes a constraint. We are impatient to shake off the demands of others and, at the same time, wary of the years ahead, knowing that it must have more meaning than daily golf and nightly talk shows or we will indeed fall into stagnation and despair.

The gift hidden in physical aging is discovering that life is more than accomplishment, more than doing and success. Halftime movement spokesperson Lloyd Reeb, in his book of the same title, called it moving "from success to significance." I suspect we need some experience of success in the world before we are ready to look beyond that for more meaning. As in the creation story, maybe we need to know "it is good" before we can enter into the ambiguity of later life, of consciously knowing good and evil, darkness and light, failure and success, beginnings and endings as the rhythm of renewal that is built into creation. I find that paradoxical realm a creative soup for spiritual completion and satisfaction. That's the terrain I want to explore.

Erikson's stages of development provide a good place to start. He defined generativity as what we pass along to our children, but from the 1960s onward, other writers expanded Erikson's work with theories of lifelong learning. We began to hear terms such as "giving back" and "giving forward" for these later years, while scientific research detailed the amazing plasticity of our brains to make new connections as we age. What we thought was fixed and deteriorating turns out to be flexible and creative. At the same time, psychiatrist Carl Jung's pioneering work with memories, dreams, and reflections gave us a framework for aging as a journey of consciousness and integration. Generativity took on a broader meaning, that of recognizing our connection with the wider world and living into that knowing.

As I interviewed people for this book about this new phase of active life, some of the questions I heard focused on these connections: "What is this generative period for? Why are we alive now, with these social and spiritual assets? What kind of a world do we want? What kind of a world do we want for our children? Our grandchildren?" Others were more focused on the personal: "What piece of this picture belongs to me? What am I here for? What is my call now?"

As I approached the possibility of retirement myself, it was the third round of call, "What is my unique gift?" that interested me more and more, and I began to realize that understanding how I moved through the previous rounds of call in my life would help me grapple with this familiar, yet new, question. A spiral never returns to exactly the same point, although we may feel a similar pattern in each round. Although there is a certain developmental quality to these rounds of call—asking "Who am I?" in our twenties and thirties, "What is my true work?" in our forties and fifties, and, "What is my unique gift?" in our sixties and beyond—the questions are not limited to any age. Any or all of these questions may return in each round. However, for the sake of definition, I want to describe the distinctive qualities of each round of call separately.

Round 1: Identity

In the early years of adulthood, we discover our skills and build a strong enough ego to leave the magnetic field of our parents. Many of us also find someone to pair with, to make a new home, and we discover how hard it is (especially for women) to preserve our separate selves in the midst of the strong pull toward merger or fusion. If we can maintain the "otherness" of the other, marriage creates an opportunity to know ourselves as loved and capable of loving another. One man said to me, "I didn't know that I could be loved for myself until she loved me, warts and all. Knowing that gave me the ground for my personhood." Others achieve that sense of a separate self on their own or in the context of their work. Psychologists identify this stage as autonomy and intimacy, but in the wider realm of call, it is a time of discovering that our individual lives have a purpose and direction, that we have the power to make moral decisions and to live with the results.

But the search for identity is not limited to young adulthood. Each time we make a major shift, we revisit these early identity questions. Now, as we age, many of us are living beyond the definition of a career. Our new questions are: "Who am I without a title, a parking space, a regular paycheck? Who am I now that my wife is disappearing into the fog of dementia? Now that my body is changing? Now that my partner has died?"

If we have been defined by a job, the end of that structure will free us to find ourselves more fully. If we have been defined by a primary relationship, absence may be the beginning of a new day. If we have been defined by our physical appearance or capabilities, we will need to find a new identity that fits with the reality of who we are now.

I think of a retreat I was leading where I drew the attention of the group to the altar cloth, with its requisite candle and flowers, that was spread on the center of the floor. I asked people to think of their lives as a journey away from the home of their parents (a journey of exile) and then back toward center, where, as American poet Robert Frost wrote, "the Secret sits" (a journey of return). Then I asked them to slip off their shoes and place them somewhere in the room to signify where they were on this journey of exile and return. As you might expect, there were shoes everywhere. Some people even placed their shoes outside the room, on the porch. One older woman put hers close to the altar cloth, pointed outward. When I asked her about it, she said: "I've just barely left home. I went from my parents' home into marriage. It was more of the same. But my husband died, and I'm just beginning the journey to know who I am."

What courage she had to name her place, to step into the risk of a new identity at this time in her life. But what better time? When I asked each person to choose a name for herself, she chose Explorer. And when she picked an object to symbolize her journey, she chose a giant magnifying glass—"so I can see little things more clearly." She was ready to find a new identity, a scheme of self-understanding that was finally her own.

Embracing this first round of call needs to happen again and again, as part of a spiral of change, flexibility, and adjustment. We need to claim who we are *now* if we are to be generative rather than rigid, bitter, and despairing that we have failed to withstand the relentless press of time. I remember, as a young adult, how being married raised questions of identity for me. Was I more than Mrs. Peter Bankson? Was I still Marjory Zoet, too? Was I more than a teacher, a friend, an American? I remember seeing the first pictures of the earth from space and feeling another shift in my identity. I had a sense of wonder that the world was so small and that I was a living part of the lovely blue-green web of life. Could I say with confidence that I was a child of God and part of God's ongoing creation? The next phase of my professional life was easier. I could identify myself as a potter, and then as president of Faith At Work (now called Lumunos) and editor of its magazine *Faith@Work*.

These questions of identity arise again and again. As we age, we wonder whether we have something to contribute to the well-being of the world, wherever we may be in it. When I retired from Faith At Work, redesigning my business card required more thought. How would I identify myself now? Finally I settled on these words: "artist," "author," and "seasoned spiritual guide."

Our spirituality takes us beyond the external associations of family, clan, and tribe to a wider realm of belonging. This is our quest for meaning and purpose as we age, our search to find the place where we belong. The identity round of call invites us to continually discover and rediscover ourselves in a larger story, in God's creation story.

Round 2: Vocation

As adults, the spiral of call moves quickly from identity to the question of work and vocation. More than a job, our *vocare*, our real work, is an expression of who we are and why we are here. Yes, we work for money, and that is part of the satisfaction that comes in the stage of career consolidation. Yet, for many, paid employment is more of a duty than an expression of soul. Finding work that fits who we are and what we can do is also a spiritual practice, a call from God as we mature and take on the responsibilities of adulthood.

At every age, I believe there is some particular work in the physical world that is ours to do. It may be the job we are being paid for. It may be what we do at home, out of public sight, to care for a disabled child or an aged parent. It could be the art we create on weekends, or the effort to change the conversation at a policy conference. Call makes the bridge between our skills and our work. Call is the element that brings meaning to what we do every day. At each transition stage of life, we need to revisit the questions of vocation: "What am I to do now? What is my work in this place? Where can I begin? With whom? What is the inner work I now have time to do? What are my dreams telling me? What does my body want?"

Notice that the identity questions of the first round of call are mostly *being* questions—"Who *am* I?"—while the vocation questions of this second round are *doing* questions. They typically begin with *what, how,* and *when,* and they focus around our skills, gifts, values, and desire for family and community. Embracing the second round of call in our generative years means rethinking our *doing*—retirement or non-retirement. Our questions are questions of movement: "What is my work *now*? What are the gifts I was born with? The skills I've developed? How do I fit with others? What is my work *tomorrow*? Who are my people? What is my particular contribution? What shall I do with my 'one wild and precious life'?" as the poet Mary Oliver says.

I see work as something we will do throughout our lives, even though the form may change from one decade to the next. Although our talents usually determine what we've chosen as a career, what we're good at may not be the whole story. In fact, I'm pretty sure that our skills can get in the way of exploring the unknown parts of our lives, both inward and outward. The drive to excel, to be recognized and rewarded financially, is a powerful and time-consuming force that keeps us tied to feedback from others.

People in our youth-oriented culture seem fixated on success, be it financial or using our training and education for special recognition. I suspect that busyness, speed, and a cult of newness keep us tied to the expectations of others and distract us from the inner work of knowing what actually makes us feel satisfied. Until we can turn off our cell phones and pagers and listen for the deeper currents of human connection, we will keep running, keep watching for external signs of success.

As our journey outward begins to slow down, the journey inward can pick up—if we consciously pursue generativity rather than simply putting in time. When we have more time and energy to spend on discovery, we can either spend it in front of the television set or turn the thing off in favor of writing and reflecting. The extrovert may not take up journaling or dream work but instead find insight from engaging with different kinds of people than she worked with during her career. The introvert may not start a center for homeless women but find that he can befriend a child with special needs.

Nothing is ever set in stone. Our postcareer work may look different from what we've done with our skills at an earlier time, in our thirties and forties. If we've spent years in front of a computer, our work now may be physical—gardening, potting, manual labor on a pilgrimage trip. If we've spent a career in the classroom, it may be time to quilt, to paint, to take jazz piano lessons, to be a learner again. And if we've been immersed in creative arts, it may be time to learn the lexicon of numbers and forms. In the generative period, our work will be less defined by outward measures of success and recognition and more defined by an inward sense of satisfaction and rightness.

Round 3: My Unique Gift

If we're fortunate, the outer work that we have done in our forties and fifties will provide an economic and experience base for the third round of call—one that can be more experimental and adventuresome—exploring more fully the question, "What is my unique gift?"

We may have addressed this question at an earlier stage in life, but each spiral of call takes us deeper into the knowledge of who we are and why we are here. Those questions will never be answered definitively, completely, but if we continue to attend to the questions of identity and vocation for this productive span of years between sixty and seventy-five or eighty, we are likely to discover our *charism*.

Charism is an archaic word that describes the unique gift of who we are, the character or soul we are born with. The Greek root of the word is "gift of God's grace." *Charism* is not earned or schooled; it is given to be explored and developed, not harnessed and driven for success. *Charism* is commonly thought to be a special gift, something that certain people have for drawing others to them. We sometimes speak of a charismatic leader or a charismatic personality, but in truth, we each have a *charism*, a gift we are called to bear in the world. It defines who we are and how we relate to others. It is that magnetic field that attracts and repels others. We can feel it, but not measure it. When we are in the presence of someone who is deeply at home in his own skin, with all his frailties and talents, we know it—if we are in tune with our own warmth and aliveness. At the core of creative aging is the discovery of our true gift, the DNA of our soul, which must be expressed whether we are paid for it or not.

In the story of Moses, I would say that his *charism* was his relationship with God. That's what made it possible for him to continue leading his ungrateful followers for forty years in the wilderness and continue to do it even when he knew that he would not enter the Promised Land. Without that *charism*, I suspect Moses would have turned into a bitter old man, defeated because his hopes were dashed in spite of his heroic faithfulness. But with that *charism*, Moses was able to handle the disappointment of getting a glimpse of the Promised Land, but not setting foot there. As he aged, Moses never did become the religious leader that his brother, Aaron, was. He never did become the celebrant, beloved by his people, that his sister, Miriam, was. Instead, Moses got quieter, more inward about his relationship with God. There were no more mountaintop retreats, no second edition of the Ten Commandments, no more miracles of manna or water in the dry desert. In his third round of call, Moses let go of doing all the decision making and learned to walk with God. He also learned to wrestle with God and bargain with God on behalf of his people. As German poet Rainer Maria Rilke writes,

"This is how he grows: by being defeated, decisively, by constantly greater beings."

Often a third round of call in the generative period arrives with a hint of death on its breath. Until that happens, we unconsciously act as though we and our loved ones will live forever. Glimpsing our mortality (in the form of illness or death of a loved one) is a wake-up call, an invitation to dig deeper, explore unknown parts of our lives. When we know that the shadow of death will never be far away, that unalterable fact gives this generative period depth, rounding out the form of who we are.

The third round of call means coming home to our full selves. Jung identified the period in our fifties and sixties as a *metanoia*, a time of rebirth linking the ego with the archetypal self. Jungians would say that creative aging is a time to explore the shadow side of ourselves that we have often projected onto others. In other words, this generative period is not so much about fulfilling our potential as it is about filling out our psychic wholeness and discovering our place in the larger scheme of things. This is the work Jung called "individuation," or conscious integration. It is a time of engaging both our gifts and our inferior functions to embrace the fullness of who we are in the world. Creative aging involves mustering the courage to live this fullness without compartmentalizing our lives.

As Parker J. Palmer, founder of the Center for Courage and Renewal, writes in *Let Your Life Speak*, we must finally learn to live "divided no more." We can let the mask go, release the power that the expectations of others has had on us. There is a wholeness, a fullness of character that comes from embracing our hidden parts, our secret dreams, our old wounds (and new ones), and the realities of our situation in a new work that is more expressive of our true self, of the soul we were born with.

Pattern of Change

Within each round of call, there is a predictable pattern of transition. Knowing the pattern is like having a map with familiar landmarks on it. Understanding this pattern can help orient us in time and space. Using the pattern as a map, we can spot transit points and anticipate feelings of sorrow and loss, or plan for unproductive periods. I have found that it helps to know where I am in the process because then I'm not as scared or as likely to stop the process altogether. Even though I still have to walk the trail, I can get my bearings and feel as if I'm headed in the right direction.

The pattern of each round is simple. When we come to a transition point in our lives, the next round of call must begin with an ending, closure for something that we were already doing. Usually, release and closure begin to happen internally before we are ready to announce our departure. Then we move to an ambivalent middle period, when things become uncertain, like the cocoon stage of a butterfly, and we're not sure what's going to come next. Only then do we arrive at the visible starting point, a new beginning.

Understanding that every new phase of life begins with an ending—with grief and loss—runs counter to what we've been taught about progress and growth. We Americans are impatient. We tend to think that trying harder will produce results faster, and that there's some reward for arriving first. But in the spiral of call, we need to take our metaphors from nature. Autumn signals the end of summer fruitfulness. Colors turn and leaves drop in a sure sign that winter is coming. Winter looks barren, neutral, dead. Winter is a spare season to the eye, while underground seeds are readying to sprout. Hibernation and gestation intertwine, preparing for a new season of growth. Finally, spring comes and newness appears.

In his classic book *Transitions: Making Sense of Life's Changes*, internationally known author, speaker, and consultant William Bridges uses the predictable pattern found in nature to describe the way people make major changes. We must begin with endings, he notes, followed by the ambivalence of a neutral zone, before we can arrive at the new beginning we imagined. I believe this three-part pattern of internal transformation is a rhythm that we all experience, consciously or unconsciously, each time we come to a new round of call.

From my observation, experience, and interviews, I believe that each of Bridges's periods has two distinct phases.

Endings involve both release and resistance:

- Release: letting go of the vocational identity associated with our career or primary work.
- Resistance: feeling stuck, stagnant, resisting change.

A new round of call at the generative stage of life typically begins with physical signs of age. Diminishment and loss of mobility become more obvious. Death comes to stay somewhere in our experience, and we recognize that our choices matter because our physical bodies are finite. Autumn signs abound. Life itself will come to an end, our bodies tell us. The inner reality of release and resistance begin the process, flashing a warning signal to stop, look, and listen to our lives. In fact, we may need to pause and regroup, get our bearings in the realities of body and soul at this stage of life. Some repairs may be needed. There may be relationships to mend, endings to acknowledge, and adjustments to be made before we can begin something new with a whole heart.

The neutral zone churns with gifts from the past and hints of the future:

- Reclaiming: drawing energy from the past, discovering unused gifts.
- Revelation: forming or finding a vision of the future.

The neutral zone is winter for the soul. Although this is a time when nothing seems to be happening on the outside, much is stirring on the inside. It may seem that stagnation has set in. We may feel as if we are going in circles between reclaiming, which looks back, and revelation, which looks forward. The neutral zone is a night sea journey, a time to troll the unconscious for images, signs, and wonders while the ego sleeps.

Then there is what I call a crossing point, where we move from stagnation to generativity. Before this point, the phases are almost entirely internal. The decision to embrace a new identity, a new call, is like a river crossing and marks a major passage from feelings of stagnation to actual generativity. It takes courage and clear purpose. It requires that we leave some things behind—old habits, old fears, even old friends, as we make the passage to a new form of work. The call that has been forming slowly is now ready to take shape in the world. It is a time to wake up. This brings us to the point of visible new beginnings.

The two phases of new beginnings make the change visible to others:

- Risk: stepping out into the world with a new vision.
- Relating: finding or creating new structures for a new kind of work.

This is the period when our new sense of identity is expressed in the world. Risk is springtime for the soul. It may come in fits and starts. A pocket of buds burst into bloom too early and is nipped by frost. Then a hillside blooms, and we know we have arrived fully in a new season. Whatever we have held close, afraid to expose to others, now seems ripe and ready to share. Relating describes the connection between shared vision and common enterprise.

Although not everyone will experience the pattern of transformation precisely in this order, the issues they represent need to be addressed as we move from the vocational identity we have had in midlife to the generative period that follows.

As you rethink retirement—or non-retirement—in this changing world, I hope these patterns of transition will invite you to release your identity of the past; acknowledge resistance and learn from it; reclaim old interests and passions; welcome wonder and revelation; sense the right time to act; risk creative newness; and build relationships to give your call form and substance. Out of new beginnings, hope is reborn. Gladness returns, and you can find a measure of peace and challenge in this new season of life.

2

RELEASE
The Inner Work of Leaving

For everything there is a season,
and a time for every matter under heaven.
—Ecclesiastes 3:1

The first signs of autumn always come as a surprise. It's suddenly dark when I leave the house for my morning walk. The rain has a chill in it. A gust of wind sends a flutter of leaves down before the first frost comes. Fall is a season of release, a harbinger of completion and closure, of harvest and preparation for the barrenness of winter.

Everything, including our work in the world, has its own life cycle. Work that was once life giving and productive begins to feel oppressive, demanding, even impossible. Tempers flare. Patience wears thin. Our bodies feel tired, driven, stressed. We long for rest and relief, but a day off or even a vacation doesn't provide the renewal we want. That's a sure sign we are coming to the end of a longer cycle and need to consider how to plan for a good transition.

In many ways, our culture denies the need for endings, both personal and institutional. We avoid good-byes and tend to regard endings as failure. Even planned retirement is tinged with the fear of economic stricture. In the current economic climate, there is plenty of blame and little discussion of seasonal rhythms, natural cycles of work and rest. Instead, we focus on low ratings, financial mismanagement, and loss as though life is meant to be a continual push for success.

Recognizing when a career has run its course has both an inner and an outer dimension. Some people know it's time to move on, but the institution isn't ready yet. Others are summarily dismissed before they have done the inner work of release. If we are to make a healthy transition from a challenging career into a different kind of work that is both satisfying and needed, we need to pay attention to the dynamics of closure in order to make space for new growth. Like leaves falling from a tree in autumn, release is part of creation's story. One phase must end so another can begin.

In the pattern of transition, release is the first of two ending phases. Release requires that we rework our identity associated with our career or primary role. We must detach from the image that we hold of ourselves through our vocation. Perhaps we give up the title or a parking place or a corner office. We may need to turn in the computer, give back the keys, receive a last paycheck. We may smile graciously and listen while others praise our work but feel empty inside. The task of release involves making peace with what has or has not been accomplished. We need to acknowledge that the time and opportunity for making a difference in the world through our work will never be repeated in exactly the same way.

Signs of the End

"I'm always tired," she sighed at the end of our conversation. "Carrying all the variables just weighs me down." After twenty-five years as pastor of a large suburban church, Laura could see the fruits of her ministry: a full church bustling with outreach ministries; two Sunday services and a Saturday night coffeehouse service; a popular youth program; regular mission trips to South Africa; and a string of younger pastors whom she had mentored into mature ministry over the years. Now another change in staff had triggered her thoughts about when to retire. "I don't know if I have the energy to do this again," she acknowledged.

Although she looks fit and healthy, Laura is graying at the temples and will be sixty-five this year. Her congregation knows that she will probably be retiring in the next three to five years, but is it time to say those words now? Because the personnel committee will be wrestling with the budget and questions around hiring a new associate, is this the time to make the move? How will she know when it's time to go? And what will she do with the experience she has gained?

At some level, Laura knows that her inner guidance is preparing her public self for departure. She worries, writes in her journal, talks with her spiritual director, and tries to keep her growing sense of completion from slipping out inadvertently. She is self-aware enough to know there is some danger of making a "Freudian slip" about her intentions, and she feels some urgency to decide when and how to announce her retirement so the church can plan for her transition along with finding a new associate.

Laura has always depended on prayer for inner guidance, but she is finding it more and more difficult to carve out time for silence, for discernment at the very time she needs it most. The external pressures are increasing to a point of desperation. She has always said that she wanted to go to South Africa and work in the orphanage that their previous mission trips had helped build, but now she has a dearly loved grandchild nearby. When I asked what she might do locally, she admitted she'd like the job of one of her associates: "I'd like to work part-time for the church—do pastoral care and small group ministry—let somebody else handle the overall planning."

Releasing a position that has been satisfying and challenging for the past twenty-five years, and a career that stretches back more than forty years, is a process that will take longer than the simple decision that it's time to retire. Her identity has been intertwined with her professional role, and she has much to be proud of. In some ways, that will make release even harder. Yet as the pressures of her work seem to tighten their grip on her time and energy, her ministry is no longer flowing freely from her heart. She recognizes that the joyfulness that used to buoy her spirit in the midst of ceaseless demands on her time seems to be more fleeting, less reliable. For her, it is a sign that the end is coming. She is already beginning to do the internal work of deciding how and when to make public her intuition that she is coming to the end of her career.

Having an image of what she would like to do next gives Laura a sense of forward motion. Even if she does not ultimately move to part-time work doing pastoral care and small group ministry, imagining the next phase of her journey helps her contemplate releasing the current phase. Like the proverbial trapeze artist, picturing another bar swinging toward her as she thinks about when to let go of the one she's been holding reassures her that there is a future for her beyond this job.

The intuition that we have come to the end of a work that has been deeply satisfying and challenging is hard to acknowledge. The signs may be there for a long time before we are willing to pay attention. We may see external pressures as simply challenges that we have to meet—until our bodies rebel, our hearts seize up, or our joints stiffen. Internal signals that a work has run its course may eat away at us, leading to depression or chronic frustration. We may feel lost, abandoned by the very purpose that once was so compelling, and yet unable to move because we have nowhere else to go. That space can be desolate and lonely. Our dreams may be troubled; our thoughts jumbled, distracted, or fantasy-laden. We may have trouble concentrating because the task at hand no longer engages our soul. Or perhaps we'll choose to "put in our time" until we reach a particular retirement goal. But as the story of Moses reminds us, to move forward we first have to "get out of Egypt." We need to find release from the hold that our work has had on us.

In the face of such pressure, our culture tends to focus on better self-care. We look to physical exercise, taking regular time off, therapy, and vacations to relieve the pressure and sustain the effort. But if the dilemma is really a spiritual question, we may actually need to let the tension deepen until the inner taskmaster that is driving us to meet our obligations (or whatever we tell ourselves that keeps us on the job) is ready to release us from work that has become bondage.

If our vocational path has been motivated by a greater cause—feeding the hungry or housing the homeless, for example—it may be particularly hard to release our work and be open to a new call that doesn't seem as grand or as noble. If we have been captivated by a greater purpose or simply attracted by the power of working for an organization with wide influence, then release will also feel like a loss of our ideals.

Understanding this tension as part of discovering the creative source of a new call—rather than the unwanted curse of aging—can make a huge difference between despair and hopefulness. If we understand that release is necessary before something new can develop in our lives, and if we allow ourselves to sense that God is at work to open a way through, we can hold the tension firmly but lightly, alert and waiting for the right time to act.

Ready or Not

Release is never as simple as it sounds. To leave an organization where we have been comfortable and affirmed is not easy because it means letting go of the title, role, perks, and salary that came with the position. We must leave the environment of power and productiveness represented by an organization that is bigger than our individual efforts. When we leave, we may take a few symbols with us, but often we are left feeling naked, a "nobody" once again. We all know people who spend the rest of their lives recounting "war stories" from the years when they were in the thick of the fray, whether that was the marketplace or a scholarly library.

The timing of release may not be in our control. Sometimes we aren't the ones who determine that a particular work is coming to an end. The span of our work may be determined by an organization or a company, or we may be fired or summarily replaced. Buyouts and corporate mergers can make this transition brutal and unexpected. We all know people who have been told to clear their desks and leave by the end of the day. That's when the realities of age and expectation make transition the hardest. Mandatory retirement can be planned for, but the current economic reality of uncertain pension funds and fluctuating investments have created a climate of fear that makes rigid or unexpected endings seem draconian. Nevertheless, endings arrive whether we want them or not, and the issue is whether we will be taken over by fear, with its attendant stasis and stagnation, or whether we will find a way through our shock and fears to some new place where life can be sweet again.

For people who are suddenly fired, finding a way to release feelings of failure or humiliation can be difficult. But it can also open the doorway to greater self-understanding and wholeness. Often, by the time we have come to the end of a challenging career, we are utterly worn out from meeting the demands of others. We have had little time to spend in reflection and no time for noticing more subtle hints of a new direction. The shock of displacement is sometimes enough to break through our patterns of self-sufficiency or weary acceptance of "what is." It may initiate a time when we seek out a spiritual director or return to the sacramental mysteries of the church.

After many years of working in information technology, Jeff was suddenly without a job when his division was simply dropped. In public, he talked over and over about being fired. He had wanted to work until he could draw the maximum Social Security payment, but now he would either have to find another job or learn to live on less. He seemed absolutely stuck, unwilling to learn a new system that would make him more employable and unable to detach from his former identity.

Jeff turned to his spiritual director for guidance and was surprised when she suggested that he might gain a wider perspective by reading Saint Teresa of Avila's *The Interior Castle*. That was definitely not his style or preference. His director suggested that he read slowly and imagine himself in each of the seven mansions described by this sixteenth-century mystic. Although the language seemed strange and archaic, he found himself drawn in by Teresa's visual imagery. Her description of the first mansion, with its different forms of humility, unlocked the gate of Jeff's heart. The anger and hurt he was carrying began to soften as he did the daily exercises of active imagination. He discovered that he could feel loved and held by a divine presence. With the wisdom that comes from long experience, his spiritual director had seen the potential for serious study and openness to the spirit that Jeff had not seen in himself.

The most noticeable result of this interior shift for Jeff was that he stopped his repetitive recital of his job loss. He began volunteering to help with his church's website and has now decided that he wants to know more about spiritual direction, to help others who find themselves in the same distress he was in. Having some inkling of a new role for himself has helped him release his hold on his former job as his primary identity. An inner sense of being loved by God—not for what he does but for who he is—has already begun to transform him from the inside out.

Disorienting or Liberating?

If discovering our call is a lifelong inner process of discovering who we are *now*, then the work we do at each stage of life will hopefully be an expression of our values and our particular skills. But if we keep growing internally, we will continually outgrow the roles and structures that define us in public. Like crustaceans, we outgrow our organizational shells and need to shed them, even when that leaves us feeling naked and unprotected. Release at this stage can be both liberating and disorienting.

For people who have changed jobs or careers several times in their lives, their previous experience of shifting from one form of work has already given them some practice in learning from another change at the generative stage.

My husband, Peter, benefitted from this kind of adaptation by being able to retire the first time at age forty-two, after twenty-one years in the army. Because many people retire from military service at a relatively young age, releasing his identity was not really difficult.

His contributions were acknowledged, and we enjoyed a final celebration with friends. With his ethos of service, Peter expected to contribute something of value to society with a second career. "I wanted something that would build a better society and use my skills in a new way," he said.

With a modest retirement income, Peter essentially had a sabbatical after twenty-one years of concentrated work, which allowed him to shift his priorities and consider where he wanted to invest himself. He was able to test several options before he settled in at Communities In Schools (CIS), a national school drop-out prevention program. By the time he turned sixty, he was proud to wear a funny hat with his official CIS title: GRIM (Government Relations and Information Management). He had found ways to bring a variety of different skills and experiences to CIS during a period of rapid expansion.

But by the time he was sixty-five, Peter was ready to retire again. Changes in office structure and his own restlessness made it a good time to celebrate the completion of his work with CIS and move on. We realized that he had been mildly depressed for about a year before he decided it was time to leave. Once he made the decision to release his work at CIS, his energy began to return. In retrospect, his sense of depression was a sign that it was time to make a change, to leave the organizational structure that had mirrored back to him much about his value and worth to society.

When there is a good fit between the work we do and who we are, retirement can seem like a death experience. We no longer know who we are and where we belong when we leave the familiar patterns of the workplace. But if we understand depression or disquiet as a sign that we have outgrown the persona that that organization requires, then we can let it go, trusting that some new expression of who we are at this age is already growing inside.

Changing the work context can be liberating and profoundly disorienting at the same time. For Peter, releasing his career at CIS proved to be more difficult than his retirement from the army, because he had invested more of himself at CIS. In addition to his official role, he had often functioned as an unofficial chaplain at CIS, listening to people's concerns and helping them find a way to align their inner and outer needs. It was that role that proved to be more difficult to release, but in it, he discovered the seeds of his next work.

One reason Peter could initiate his retirement from CIS was that it was not his only mirror of identity. In the background, there was another nourishing stream in Peter's life that began flowing more strongly as he made more space and time for it by leaving employment at CIS. He joined a church leadership team of four people, which not only offered one-day-a-week employment for a small stipend but also gave him a place where his collegial style and temperament could be affirmed. This helped sustain his spirit through the radical adjustment of releasing the professional identity he had built at CIS. This new work also gave him a position to "age in place," where he could experience continuity and creativity with new team members who would join and leave over the years to come.

Stagnation or Vision?

At the age of fifty-seven, Gordon Cosby, the founder and pastor of Church of the Saviour, an innovative ecumenical congregation in downtown Washington, D.C., began to preach and write about the increasing complexity of new missions that were facing this growing church. He was quite clear that he did not feel called to be the head of a burgeoning organization, and his deep prayer life gave him the confidence to preach to the edge of his understanding. He refused the cultural model of bigger is better and did not cling to the presumed mandate of a good shepherd—to keep his flock together. Instead, as the church grew, he was willing to release the structure that he had created.

By the time he was fifty-nine, Gordon issued a clarion call to disband the existing church structure and form smaller units based on separate missions. It was a revolutionary vision. His willingness to let go of the original church structure helped him frame the subsequent disbursement of the church community as more like an exodus from Egypt. Gordon was able to give his congregation a sense of larger purpose and the promise of spiritual guidance from others beyond himself. His willingness to let go of centralized leadership gave other people the courage to claim their own call to leadership, and five separate congregations eventually formed out of the original church body.

In the thirty years since that time, four more lively congregations have formed, each with a different character and a different mission. Gordon's willingness to release his position as the CEO of a burgeoning bureaucracy made room for a second generation of leaders to emerge, and it also freed him to continue experimenting with new forms of "being church." Unlike most church-growth experts, Gordon consistently refused to speculate about the future. His vision was not about structure or doctrinal purity. Instead, his vision was one of discovery and relationship with God. For him, release of the old form was simply the next step, and he was willing to live with the chaos and consternation of others in order to do that.

Good Courage

Although leaving a field that we have loved can be disorienting, even if we deeply desire this release, letting go of the primary identity that we have established over thirty or forty years of effort is a big decision requiring enormous shifts inside. We may lose our sense of place and direction. Some people hang on to an old identity because they are simply too frightened to change. It takes courage to leave a known role and step into the unknown.

If, like Moses, we hold a larger story of divine presence and call, we will be able to recognize the signs that it is time to leave and find the courage to take the next step. God had warned Moses and his people that their exit from Egypt would not be easy. Pharaoh would harden his heart and refuse to let the Israelites go, and God would send ten plagues, each more terrible than the last, until finally the Pharaoh would change his mind. The final plague was the death of the firstborn sons in Egypt. In a ritual act of passage into a new life, Moses instructed his people to smear blood on the doorpost as a sign to the angel of death that this house should be spared. Thus the Hebrews were "marked" for safe passage out of Egypt. In our Judeo-Christian tradition, the yearly ritual of celebrating Passover honors the possibility that we have been chosen to leave, selected for another mission and protected during departure. It is an important message to carry when we leave a position we have claimed for many years. The story of Passover resonates with many departure rituals because it reminds us of the courage it takes to leave.

Joan had been an Episcopal priest for more than thirty years. When she started seminary, ordination in the Episcopal Church was not even possible for women. Throughout her career, she faced both prejudice and opportunity. She believed that her call to ordained ministry came from a source beyond herself, and she faced its challenges with courage and perseverance. Like many of her cohorts, she had a love-hate relationship with the institutional church as the structures slowly shifted to accept women in authority.

In parish ministry, Joan chose multiple staff situations because she wanted to balance family and work rather than be consumed by a career in the church. With her doctorate in pastoral counseling, she found that she was able to find satisfying work within the larger institutional structure of the denomination. But then, as she came to the age when the pension fund would supplement Social Security, she was nervous about letting go of her position. It had given her a place to stand in her marriage to a highly successful entrepreneur, and her clerical collar had given her another kind of credibility in the world. She recognized and valued the institutional identity that she had fought so hard to achieve.

Joan is unusually conscious of the deeper meaning of Eucharist, understanding that this sacrament of bread and wine is the promise of new life rising out of death. How to trust that message of hope was another question, one that she had to live her way into. "I know that when I celebrate Eucharist, I am giving public recognition to the promise of death and resurrection," she said, "but now I'm having trouble believing that it will happen for me."

As she prepared to leave her position of administering a grant to support young clergy residents at her church, Joan worked to fund the program into the future, and then she set a firm departure date with her supervisor. She kept naming her fears to her spiritual director and gathering her courage for the immediate next steps that she had to take. "I'm walking through this by faith," she said, "not by sight."

Structuring her departure was another way that Joan took charge of her fears. She worked for two weeks with the new director and said personal good-byes to the mutual ministry teams she had worked with. On her last Sunday, she attended all three services at the church, thanking the congregation at each service and receiving their prayers of blessing. She said later that it felt like a mutual blessing, heartfelt and satisfying. She also gathered a circle of personal friends who had supported her journey of ordained ministry to thank them as well. What she realized as the process unfolded was that she was not only saying farewell to her position, but she was also releasing her vocation as a priest.

After all that it had cost her to gain her place as a priest, leaving her position was a test of will and stamina. Once Joan had completed her process of release, she discovered that her sense of priesthood remained, that it was not as tied to having a position in the church as she had thought. She has come through the ordeal feeling whole and blessed for whatever lies ahead.

Good Closure

Learning to say good-bye is an important part of release, and it can be made even harder if we are leaving a company we have formed ourselves, or a movement we have started. Initiating something and then building it faithfully over time can lead to deep internal identification with the organization and make the process of separating more difficult because it requires that we tease apart our sense of self from a sense of accomplishment.

Jackie had been running a therapeutic center for learning-disabled kids for nearly twenty-five years. Her state-of-the-art center combined physical stimulation and quieting techniques with learning goals, and her work was the standard for other specialists in the area. She had trained many younger therapists and enjoyed both reputation and financial reward for her work. Her daughters were grown now, and there was a new man in her life. When she arrived at my class on the subject of discerning call, she said, "I don't know if it's time to renew the lease for my center or not. I'm hoping this class will help me decide." The external question of whether to renew the lease linked with her inner sense of changing seasons in her life.

Like most important decisions, this one was not simple. To close her practice would mean leaving client parents and children stranded without the learning support she had provided. Her business acumen had also provided good jobs for other people. "I used to be the only resource in town," Jackie said, "but now there are others. Some of my competition trained with me and have started their own businesses." Income was another factor. Her future, another. The presenting question—whether to sign a three-year lease or not—was just the tip of the iceberg.

As the class worked its way through the seven-phase pattern of change that we experience at each round of call, Jackie did her inner work, paying attention to the signs that were coming her way. But everything seemed stuck; nothing was flowing.

By the end of the class, Jackie was clear that she was not going to sign a new lease, but the decision to close her business still seemed too much for her. I suggested that if she knew she would not continue in that place, maybe she could focus on good closure at their current location with her staff. She looked a little surprised and then relieved: "Good. That gives me something specific to do."

Without jumping to the long-term question of whether to close her business, Jackie could focus on the immediate question and could make the decision not to sign the lease. That freed her to prepare her staff to leave that place, and it gave her more time to decide whether to sell or lease her business to someone else in the future, or simply to close the doors.

Jackie discovered that release could happen in manageable stages, that she did not need to decide everything at once. She gave herself time and space to value what she had put into her business and to find other ways of offering those skills to others. At this writing, she has signed up for a mission trip to Ecuador, where she will offer her therapeutic skills at a center for disabled children.

Good closure is not something that happens by itself. It takes a vision of the larger purpose and direction for the organization as well as care for the individuals who will be involved in the organization's future. Particularly if some of the current staff will be continuing while others will be released from their employment, it's important to celebrate the good things that have been accomplished together. For some, a party might be the right venue. For others, some visual presentation of benchmarks could be a way to acknowledge the contributions of different people or divisions to overall success. When people are leaving or a division is closing, it's especially important to name and acknowledge the value of their contributions. Leaders need to give the process thought and prayer, listening for the not-obvious things that need to be included. Good and timely endings are part of the process of clearing the psychic space.

There's an interesting angle to this idea of "closure" when it comes to women's work, especially if it involves a business a woman has created. For many women, their work flows in both directions, from the giver to the receiver and back again. That it never ends speaks not of drudgery, but of love and connection. It brings that eternal dimension of love into time and space with a practical gesture, a specific act, going the extra mile. This raises some complex questions: If that work is never ending, how do we know when it's finished? When is it time to move on, to change the form and venue of our work? How do we know when one round of call has been completed and another is about to begin?

If the satisfaction of a career has involved lots of heart connection, I think it is even more important to pay attention to good closure. Joan was able to use the stability of the Episcopal Church to provide structure for her release. Jackie will have a more difficult time because she is both providing the organizational structure for others and wanting to meet her own needs for closure. Doing it in stages will help her trust the inner guidance she is getting for each step. If she can move through the process one small step at a time and not panic, I believe she will see what she needs to do next. That will give her the time to do her own inner work of release as she deals with the organizational questions.

As we age, we face the reality of endings. No matter how careful we are about eating or how ardent we are about exercise, age takes a toll on our bodies, and death comes to someone close by. We are reminded of our mortality, that time and energy are limited. Autumn comes, like it or not. Colors change. Leaves drop and the wind has a hint of winter in it.

"For everything there is a season" the ancient Sage observes. Fall is a reminder that we are called, again and again, to let old forms (attitudes, roles, masks, accomplishments) die. Nature teaches us the cycle of seed, root, shoot, and fruit, but as we get more detached from the natural world, we forget the necessity for those changes. In our technological culture, it is easier to conclude that we are in control of our lives and that endings are somehow a mark of failure. But nature tells us that nothing is meant to be permanent. Daylight wanes and seasons turn; winter comes whether we want it or not. External change and internal transition are realities. Our choice is how to deal with them, whether to try and hang on to what is familiar or let go so something new can take its place.

Release is a conscious part of aging. If we put more focus on outward appearances and outward signs of success, aging will be a fearful thing and the end of our primary role in the marketplace will be mourned with regret. Retirement will represent loss of the person others think we are, and we will feel naked, unprotected, and unsure of who we are in the world. But if we choose to emphasize inward development and exploration, aging can be an invitation to savor the richness of creativity and imagination, to offer ourselves in new ways that we never had time for before.

Going through the discipline of release with courage and conscious planning means that we are more likely to live in the present moment and love the time we have. Living into the process of releasing the inner sense of who we are and the external marks of professional success means that we will pay attention to inner signs that it is time to let go of a position of power and recognition, as Laura did when she prepared to leave her church.

Reaction from an outdated identity will tend to erupt if we have been summarily fired or replaced, as Jeff was. Our culture equates *being* with *doing*, identifying us primarily by how we serve the economy. We live with the daily question from others: "And what do you do?" When that identity is stripped away without ceremony or acknowledgment, we need to find ways to bring closure. Jeff turned to a spiritual director for help. A spiritual discipline, such as entering Teresa's interior castle, may be a path for letting go of an outdated identity and discovering that we can be loved for who we are, not what we do.

Peter and Joan were both able to plan their departure from work they valued, trusting that the institutions they had worked for would continue to serve others. Peter eased into part-time work at a church while Joan worked on her house, waiting for a new understanding of what her call to the priesthood might look like in her later years. Relinquishing the outward trappings of position and power took courage and consciousness, but they were both ready and willing.

Gordon Cosby and Jackie were founders of their organizations, and both had to face the possibility that those structures would not survive their departure. After preparing his congregation for the institutional change, Gordon released his position with a challenge for a new generation of leaders to step forward. He acted on a vision of faithfulness and right timing, while Jackie took a more cautious approach, moving one step at a time. Knowing that their choices will affect many others puts extra weight on founders who care deeply about the missions of their organizations.

Ending a primary career is never easy, and releasing the identity that we have had in public is a challenge. We live in a culture that glorifies beginnings, initiative, entrepreneurship, and economic success. But recognizing that we do live with physical limits, that we must honor the realities of aging and turn our attention inward to explore the frontiers found there, is an invitation we may be reluctant to accept. Our culture says, "You can have it all." Our bodies, which are deeply rooted in the natural cycles of seasons, say, "No. There are limits. You must learn to live with limits. You must choose to let some things go in order to make space for new loves, new learnings, new life." Release is a spiritual principle, a necessary step that must be taken to let generativity emerge.

Spiritual Practice: Gratitude

Regular spiritual practices can help you delve into this generative spiral. In order to release a position or role that has provided you with a public identity, giving thanks for "what was" can be an important part of letting go.

The practice of gratitude sets a positive framework for life as a process of discovery, an adventure to be relished instead of a problem to be solved. A simple way to begin is to get a small spiral notebook and put the date on the top of each page, followed by five things you feel grateful for that day. By the end of the first week, you will notice repeats. Examine them, if you can: ask what part of that event or interaction makes you thankful. Begin to describe your gratitude more fully. Over time, this practice will draw you into the present.

Gratitude is closely tied to hopefulness, which is separate from wishfulness. Hope keeps possibility alive, and that makes space for newness. Gratitude helps you keep your eyes and ears open for divine presence and guidance in every situation. Gratitude can also help you soften the rigidity of your expectations and its inevitable corollary, disappointment. It's like spiritual yoga, asking you to breathe and stretch.

Questions to Ponder

1. Recall five endings that were significant for you. What was being completed with each ending? How did you acknowledge the importance of each one? What symbol or memento do you have of that ending?

2. How do you mark major turning points in your life today? What kind of object, such as a milestone, a cairn of rocks, or a prayer shawl, could you make to symbolize an important departure you have experienced or are contemplating?

3. Is there something in your work that still needs completion and release? What ritual or action might help you move on? Is there someone with whom you might share that release?

3

RESISTANCE
Moving Beyond Security

If you are not facing one of your tigers,
it's already eating you.
—John J. Scherer, *Five Questions That Change Everything*

At the end of a day packed with meetings, I feel restless, suspended in time. I pick up a magazine, but I can't concentrate, so I put it down again. I look at a catalog, vaguely admiring the young bodies and turning down the corners of pages I will never actually look at again. I glance at the clock. It's getting late. I should go to bed. Getting up early to walk in the morning will be hard if I don't get to sleep soon. I sip my herbal tea, waiting for the end of the newscast to tell me it's time to end the day.

When I am in the middle of a major transition, this little playlet of resistance happens nearly every night. My thinking self refuses to turn off and go to sleep. My spirit feels weary with the world's many needs, yet my mind doesn't want to rest. I have a hard time letting go of the day, as if I could squeeze some last bit of life from these final hours. In truth, some part of me fears that if I stop thinking, sloth will prevail and I will never wake up. I will have no reason to get up in the morning. I will sleep away the rest of my life. Maybe that's part of my reluctance to go to bed. But the daily rhythm of night and day can also be an assurance that morning *will* come. I will awake, but for that to happen I must enter a time of unknowing, when I am not in control.

Unknowing is fearful terrain for the modern mind. We like to plan, organize, and take charge, and yet our bodies rebel when pushed too hard, too long. Changes in our physical bodies are ushering in the next season of life. Our reflexes aren't as good as they once were. The phone directory is hard to see. We notice creaking joints in the morning as we get out of bed, or sexual impotence arrives unexpectedly. A stiff neck or a stiff back limits our lifting.

Resistance is usually the first reaction to these physical changes. Our response is to find a reason, assign a special cause, take more pills, buy a pair of magnifying glasses at the drugstore. We set a goal of reaching some former level of activity and deny these early signs of aging if we can. Our rational selves get creative about hanging on to the illusion of control by treating these changes as problems to be solved. It's a workplace habit. We automatically try to plug in the skills we have relied on in the past to deal with the unknown territory ahead.

Resistance is a natural part of the ending phase of any transition. We deny the reality of change because change feels like death. And, at a certain level, it is. As we age, our bodies are different. Our personal sense of safety feels threatened. Fear haunts the hallways of transition, fanned by ubiquitous ads on television. Our fears may focus on money (will there be enough?) or our time (what will we do if we can't work?). Worse yet, our fears may grow stronger without the bulwark of daily work demands to soothe our anxieties.

Resistance to change reminds us how difficult it can be to move into a new terrain when we don't know the geography and think we may not have an accurate map. The denial and anger stages that psychiatrist Elisabeth Kübler-Ross, author of *On Death and Dying*, described in facing death also apply to reaching the end of our primary identity in the workplace. No matter how attentive we have been to good closure, there is a residual feeling of loss, emptiness, even despair. We may feel stuck or numb. Living with resistance can seem like being stuck in molasses, and we tend to use activity to cover an uncomfortable sense of being stalled.

We knew how to meet external demands at work, so the temptation to repeat our successful strategies is strong. We all know people who trade the frantic pace of programmatic responsibilities for an equally full calendar of volunteer activities. They simply transfer a demanding career to another setting.

Yet, the more we fill our lives with external activity, the less energy we will have to give to the internal work of transition. Recovering the creative energies buried under the bedrock of public performance may take some time. A good place to begin is with the restorative power of doing nothing. Giving ourselves permission to experiment before committing to a new form of work offers us time to explore the neglected parts of ourselves and our lives.

Doing Nothing

Each night, when we let go of one day's worry and toil in order to rest, we are actually being called to trust the restorative power of doing nothing. We need to refrain from activity to remember who we are as human *beings*, not human *doings*. There is wisdom in rest—and in "wasting time" between purposeful activities.

We know that sleep is an anchor for the psyche and that sleep deprivation is a form of torture, yet our culture's insistence on 24/7 activity makes us feel guilty if we rest too much. In truth, in the larger drama of finding the generative wellspring for the next phase of our lives, we first need to let stagnation have its say. We need to attend to the wisdom of rest, of sleep, of silence and slowness, of space for *not* doing. We need to make space and time to listen at the core of our souls.

In addition to the physical necessity for nightly rest, every religious tradition invites some practice of silence, some form of meditation and prayer for spiritual renewal. While our culture fills every second with sound, our faith tradition tells us that silence heals by opening us to another realm. Like the ocean, beneath the turbulence of the surface chop, there are deeper currents full of life if we will only make space and time to go there.

A practice of daily silence may feel like static at first because it is about doing nothing. Sitting in silence, breathing, and being in a receptive mode are foreign to our habits of busyness and availability, but a contemplative practice can begin to take us beyond the brick wall of resistance.

Religious traditions also recommend setting apart one day a week to remember the larger story of which we are a part. The Ten Commandments include the admonition to "remember the Sabbath and keep it holy." As the fulcrum or hinge of the Decalogue, this commandment is different from the other, more directive "thou-shalt-nots." The word "remember" implies that we once knew this practice, but have now forgotten it and need to be reminded of our place in the greater scheme of things. To keep one day holy and set apart from the other six days of work implies that we can indeed step into another realm, a sacred space, by changing what we do with that time.

Instead, we pride ourselves on being able to multitask, juggle a thousand demands, and stay busy all the time. But with the advent of cell phones and pagers, we are in danger of slipping the moorings that can give us a sure anchor of Sabbath rest in the sea of work. In this time of instant messaging and constant connectivity, we resist disconnecting for a whole day. It seems even sacrilegious. Somehow we have made a religion of being constantly available. It is a sign of being needed, being involved and important to others, an aspect of the root impulse of *re-ligio*, which is to reconnect.

But cell phones are also a substitute for the deeper connection with ourselves that can only come in silence. Sabbath time makes space for that possibility.

Doris worked in the office of a small interfaith housing coalition. She believed in its mission and wished she had the credentials to be considered for the director's job. She was a forceful, outspoken advocate for the organization, and she identified with the low-income women who were being helped because she was once a welfare mother herself. At her age (almost sixty), she was hesitant to seek more schooling. Doris felt underpaid and underappreciated, but she didn't want to jeopardize her job because of the health insurance it provided. Her anger came out in many ways, but it was particularly directed at the new executive director who was her supervisor. The issue for Doris was complicated even further by her sense of call to this work. She felt that God had placed her there for a reason, and yet she had not been able to get over feeling enslaved by the system.

When we talked, Doris was sometimes able to see that her own mental framework of how things "ought to be" could be a trap. Loving herself and loving others was at the core of her spiritual life, but she had not been able to translate that into her relationship with her supervisor. With him, she was full of righteous indignation at what she was asked to do and, more specifically, what she was not allowed to do. Sometimes she was able to see that she had idealized her work, demanding that it provide more satisfaction than it could probably ever give her. Although she did get considerable pleasure from her volunteer activities at church, she felt stuck with no options. Doris felt she could not leave Egypt, and yet her body was telling her that she needed to make a change. She had missed a number of days at work due to illness, and her weight was going up again. Her physical health threatened to determine her future if she could not find a way to release her idealized image of how things "ought to be" in her workplace.

Then Doris was fired. Paid vacation days and health benefits through the end of the year gave her a little breathing space before she had to find another job. To her surprise, she discovered that she was relieved instead of anxious. After several encouraging interviews, she began to see her job loss as a part of her spiritual journey, an unexpected gift of Sabbath time. "I'm so loyal," she said, "I would never have left. Now I have no choice but to seek a place where my gifts and experience will be an asset rather than a liability." Although Doris did not choose this Sabbath time, she had been given space for the internal work of reconnecting with her true self, her hopes and needs for herself, and her work in the world.

To "remember the Sabbath" may seem like a strange way to address resistance and job loss, but I think it is exactly what we need to do. Although we may identify ourselves as free people, able to choose rest and renewal, our culture has really lost that sense of how to "keep it holy," how to remember our place as humans in God's larger narrative. Instead, we fill our "days off" with frantic activity and call it recreation. But holiness makes time for the whole story, something awesome and mysterious beyond ourselves. Keeping the Sabbath, no matter what day of the week it is, can be a time to remember that connection, to see our lives in a bigger context, part of a larger movement toward healing and wholeness.

Sabbath doesn't have to be boring or silent to help us remember our place in the larger scheme. We might plan a hike that is mostly silent, visit an art museum, or have a quiet meal with friends. Whatever we do, it is always good to mark the beginning and end of Sabbath time with a quiet meditation. Whether our Sabbath is a moment set aside during the day or an entire day committed to space and time for wonder, we might begin with simple attention to our breathing. The ancient practice of centering prayer is a good place to start: noticing our breath, in and out, and perhaps saying a simple mantra, such as "Be still, be at peace, here and now," can help our busy minds relax. Quickly enough, however, our inclination to solve problems will arise in the silence. I like to keep a little notebook close by to write down a word or two, then go back to breathing and sitting in silent receptive prayer to begin a Sabbath time.

Resistance thrives on constant activity. Doing nothing makes space for something else to emerge. To "remember the Sabbath" is to release our work and listen for assurance deep within.

Clues for the Future

The journey inward during this resistance phase often begins with a crisis, something that breaks through our facade of competence and self-sufficiency. Job loss, an accident, or the onset of a disabling condition may be the prompt for this transition, and we instinctively put up our defenses to the change we didn't invite. Yet if we listen to what our defensive voice is proclaiming, we may discover clues for our future. Those negative reactions, such as "I would *never* do that" or "We couldn't *possibly* live there," may be a sign of new call. At least that possibility is worth exploring.

I've learned to respect internal resistance because it means I have not really clarified what I truly need. Instead, I am probably stuck on what I *don't* want, using my energy to avoid situations that may or may not happen. I get snappish and self-absorbed, overburdened with the things I have to do. I want people to leave me alone until my nervous Nellie ego figures a way out. I know myself well enough to recognize the signs and realize that I need something else. Exploring those deeper needs before moving ahead to a new work is an important part of this resistance phase.

If we do not pay attention to those signs, our health will surely be affected over time. Our bodies may signal the need for change with a sore back, a stiff neck, or even a heart attack. Instead of treating a bodily ill simply as a sign of stress, we need to see it as an invitation to reflect on our fears and discover what our bodies are trying to convey. Resisting the realities of our bodies can be life limiting, if not life threatening. We fear the loss of physical health and capabilities. Yet we rarely ask what we want to do with our health and well-being. Learning how to accept the natural shifts in energy and capabilities, and listening to our bodies for clues to healing and wholeness is often the gateway to a new journey inward. Giving in to the realities that arrive on our doorstep can be a path through our own resistance.

Arlene was dreading retirement from her job with the local council on aging. She and her husband had little in common, and she could not imagine being at home with him all day every day. Their children lived far away, so grandparenting was not an option. Her husband had no real hobbies except singing with a barbershop quartet, and she knew they did not have the financial resources to travel.

As he approached retirement, her husband developed Parkinson's disease, and she was horrified of becoming his caretaker. From her work, she knew how the disease progressed and what they could expect; she considered leaving the marriage rather than face what lay ahead. For months she wrestled with the possibility of divorce.

Her husband had initially refused to seek help or join a Parkinson's support group at the local hospital, so Arlene was surprised when he decided to participate in an experimental three-month treatment in Arizona. Thinking that it would be good for them to get away together, she agreed to go with him. The treatment involved a series of exercises that included hearty singing to keep his lungs flexible. She participated in the program and then asked whether she could start a similar program where they lived. With the approval of the program directors, she started a chapter in their town, and the two of them have found new purpose in their life together.

In retrospect, the clue to Arlene's new call lay in her adamant resistance to caretaking. Accepting their situation rather than getting out of the marriage opened the way to new and satisfying work for Arlene and her husband. Although sorrow and loss have their place as we age, finding a way to share the basic stuff of life with others and to live with fewer distractions can enliven our love of life and our search for what matters most.

Physical Work

The flip side to the journey inward is the value of physical engagement. It can be a gateway for reconnecting with some of the forgotten parts of ourselves and our lives. Ordinary activities, such as gardening, housekeeping, cooking, and knitting, can be contemplative practices, if we do them with awareness—listening for the still, small voice of call.

For me, the path through resistance begins with physical engagement, preferably out of doors: walking each morning, yard work, and gardening. Literally pruning bushes helps me with the internal pruning I need to do. Working with clay is another source of serenity and physical engagement for me. Sometimes I need a longer time on retreat, and I hike or camp in the wilderness, alone or with others. Something that makes me physically tired helps put my ego to rest, so I can let my body begin to answer the question of "What's next?" before my mind answers with ready-made clichés. I think we have become so accustomed to comfort and predictability that we lose the edge of adventure that keeps us alive and alert. The constant effort to be safe and secure can be stultifying.

A project that will take us into unfamiliar territory with physical challenges can help us know our strengths and need for others. This can be an important pathway through the danger zone of sloth and boredom dressed up like busyness. I think of my father, who kept his balance through all the years of his medical practice by going to his holly farm on Wednesday and Saturday afternoons. He described it as "working in the dirt." Only the noise of his tractor broke the silence that was otherwise filled with breeze and birds. He never put in a phone line at the farm and could not be reached easily. To preserve those times of quiet, he arranged for others to cover for him, to deal with unexpected emergencies.

Creativity is stimulated by solving real physical problems and working with others to achieve a common goal. In our earlier years, we might have signed up for an Outward Bound experience to test ourselves and call forth the deeper wellsprings of our creativity. Now we might choose a pilgrimage or service project that will tax our strength and test our endurance, leaving us tired and grateful to be alive at the end of each day. Tolerance and teamwork with people we might not choose to spend a lifetime with can reveal unsuspected reserves and unexpected resilience for this new stage of life. It might also point to direct service as a satisfying second career.

The year after I retired as the president of Faith At Work, Peter and I offered to lead a work pilgrimage to Guatemala through the Faith At Work network. One of the board members had a connection with a good organization there, but during my years of leadership, I had not had the extra energy to organize and lead such a trip while trying to keep our nonprofit afloat. Now we could focus on how to make this an enriching experience for all the participants. I was also thinking that this trip might point me in a new direction.

The group that made this first trip included people between the ages of twenty-eight and seventy-two. Because there were no facilities to house us in the village, we stayed at a simple, safe retreat center in Antigua and drove an hour each way by bus to the work site. Peace accords to end their civil war (*la violencia*) had occurred six years before, in 1996, but United Nations observers were still on the ground to enforce the peace agreements. In the village where we arrived to dig a foundation for a primary school, families were still coming for emergency food rations to supplement food crops from the ruined fields. But the villagers, who were mostly sharecroppers working for distant landowners, had purchased a plot for the school and were eager to work with us to create a place for their children to learn. The few men left in the village were considerably more skilled at digging and hauling than we were, but our presence was a sign of interest from the outside world, and the villagers warmly welcomed us. The miracle was not turning stones into bread, but sweat equity into a school. Doing real work together made our language differences manageable, and all of us were touched by the villagers' hospitality.

For one person, the Guatemalan pilgrimage opened the pathway through resistance into a new project. Jim, a recently retired business owner, came on one of our early trips with his wife, who reported that he was becoming forgetful and bored in retirement although he was fit and enjoyed playing golf almost daily. He proved to be a cheerful traveler, a good organizer, and a hard worker on the pilgrimage. After they returned, his wife noticed his memory had improved and his interest in local service projects had increased. Now, with the economic downturn, he has gone back to work running the service department of a business he once ran as the CEO. What began as a travel adventure turned into a generative shift from living a life of full-time leisure to working part-time at something he does well. Although, initially, he resisted giving up retirement as his reward for years of constant tension, Jim discovered that he really liked working hard and organizing a job so others could participate.

Physical work on a common project is a rare experience for most Americans these days. We have used our money and technology to create vast systems where people sit before screens, tapping keys instead of shoveling dirt. Most of us on this Guatemalan pilgrimage had never tied rebar columns together with wire or mixed concrete by hand. There was something so humanly satisfying about getting to "the pour" after days of digging the foundation trench that all of us, no matter what skill or energy we'd brought, felt as if we'd accomplished a major goal together when it was done. No matter what resistances we brought with us, we all got in touch with more basic levels of cooperation and satisfaction that opened our hearts in different ways.

When life gets pared down to its simplest level, it can help us begin the conversation with larger forces beyond our control and awaken our bodies to hunger and gladness once again. The temporary condition of living together with sporadic hot water and bouts of diarrhea reminded us physically of our common humanity with others who share our world. It's not that we imagined anyone would go home from the Guatemalan pilgrimage and become a construction worker, but we believed in the human solidarity that grows out of common work, a connection that cannot be felt through a virtual experience. That, too, is a form of Sabbath.

Finding time to do nothing, to be unproductive—even playful— does not necessarily break through resistance, but it can provide breathing space to step back from the day-to-day grind and gain a larger perspective. Being fired was no holiday for Doris, but it has given her some Sabbath time to reconnect with what truly matters in her work and home life.

Accepting the realities of her husband's growing disability gave Arlene a way through her resistance. Although she deeply wanted to avoid spending the rest of her life taking care of her husband, once she decided to accompany him on his challenging journey, a way to be involved in a new kind of work that would benefit others opened for her.

Sometimes physical work provides a way to engage our bodies in the conversation about what to do with our time and energy at this stage of life. For Jim, a work project in Guatemala opened a path through his resistance to giving up what he thought he had earned, which was a lifetime of leisure. Choosing to step away from familiar patterns of doing provided a breathing space and a wider perspective for all three. It was the gift of Sabbath time and a light to see the way forward beyond the stuckness of resistance.

Spiritual Practice: Silence

Finding some quiet space in your busy life for reflection can help you move beyond resistance. Paying attention to what comes up in your thoughts or dreams can be a first step toward action. Let silence and breathing do the work.

If you can spend at least five minutes alone without distraction each morning and evening, you will begin to be more aware of your inner life. Some people light a candle and simply sit or gaze softly at a tree outside. Others sit with eyes closed, repeating a simple mantra, such as "Be here; be peace," as they breathe in and out.

Silence gives you a chance to be consciously aware of your whole self: body, mind, and soul. Sometimes the inner work is about letting go of your illusions about what life ought to be. Sometimes it is about accepting unexplored parts of yourself. Learning to pay attention to the spiritual realm that you are born with is the way through resistance to a new call. At this stage of life, the unconscious is often ready to offer guidance if your conscious mind is ready to receive it.

Questions to Ponder

1. Where do you feel stuck or resistant?

2. Is there some time in your week for the restorative power of doing nothing?

3. How might you use your Sabbath time for the internal work of listening for clues about the future?

4. Do you listen to your physical body for guidance? Is there some way that you could engage your body and then spend some time writing about whatever comes to mind?

4

RECLAIMING
Riches from the Past

For it was you who formed my inward parts;
You knit me together in my mother's womb. . . .
I am fearfully and wonderfully made.

—**Psalm 139:13–14**

Winter arrives with no warning. Increasing darkness tightens its grip on our consciousness no matter how many lights we turn on. The temperature drops, and a freezing rain strips the trees bare. Extra layers of clothing muffle movement, and a fire beckons us inside. Winter is the season for introspection, for remembering and restoration.

In the life cycle of a new call, reclaiming seeds buried in the past is the first of two phases of the neutral zone. The second phase looks toward the future, but first we must attend to needs and wants that our professional lives have pushed underground, out of our consciousness. If this period of life is to bear fruit, we must let winter do its work on the seeds of a new beginning.

During this period, we may also feel as if we are wandering around in the desert because we do not have a clear direction. It is a churning period between ending and a new beginning, between a consuming career and a new start. Old ways cling, and we obsessively replay interactions that we might have done differently. New efforts fizzle. We may feel uncreative and out of sorts. We may feel as if we are wasting time, spinning our wheels, going nowhere. Outwardly, there is little to show for our efforts. We might as well be hibernating. Stagnation seems to have settled in for the duration. It is the interior season for the soul, urging us to slow down and turn inward to reclaim energy from the past. Unused gifts may surface. Gestation is just beginning.

When I first retired from Faith At Work, other people expected me to plunge into my basement pottery studio because for a long time I had talked about wanting to do this when I had more time. But once I had more time, I didn't do it. Instead, I found myself sorting through drawers, cleaning the basement, and washing windows—preparing the space for something new. I bought cozy casual clothes and put my suits away, joined a dream group, began to exercise again. It seemed important to reclaim my body and make space for whatever was going to emerge. What I didn't realize was that the work ahead of me was to reclaim my true self, especially the less honored parts I had buried or set aside.

Parker J. Palmer, author of *A Hidden Wholeness,* describes how easily we develop a public face that is divided from the true self (or soul) we are born with. We develop the *public face* to protect our vulnerabilities. It is shaped by our interactions with others, by what gets rewarded and reinforced by success or failure. The *true self* is mute and increasingly hidden, even from ourselves. Feelings of shyness and inadequacy are simply not allowed to surface because they contradict the public persona that we show to others. When we are split this way, we literally do not know our true selves.

Positive as well as negative parts of our true self get buried. As a child, we may have loved to write or draw, create little landscapes in the mud, or weave twigs into a shelter but have long since removed ourselves from creating something with our hands. One woman showed me a collection of paper dolls that might be the germ of a new art form for her. She had pared her life down to a small apartment, but noticed that she had kept these paper dolls through every purging move and wondered what meaning they might have now.

Often, I believe, the weariness that we feel at work comes from the effort to maintain the idealized image either that we have of ourselves or that our company or colleagues have of us. As we step away from organizational structures that reinforce our public persona, this is the perfect time to reclaim our true selves. It's not that we can't do it earlier, but at this age and stage of life, we may discover that we care less about what others think and are freer to connect with and reflect our true selves. In a fundamental way, creative aging depends on reclaiming those parts of ourselves that we have disowned or denied because our very source of creativity lies in the soul, the true self.

Paying attention to the whole self is a powerful guide to inner discovery. At a recent workshop, I asked people to name the characteristics of Moses that might have been assets for his mission to lead his people out of Egypt. Some of the positive characteristics they named were a devoted and loving family, education in the palace, access to the Pharaoh, self-confidence, and a sense of justice. Then we looked at his liabilities. People quickly named his temper, that he was an outlaw in need of redemption, and that he could not speak well. Then I asked whether those liabilities could have been gifts in disguise, elements that God could use. The group saw that Moses's temper was an indication of passion. His outlaw status might have contained a longing to be with his people again and responsiveness to their suffering. And his stuttering speech gave him a bond with his brother, Aaron, as well as his dependence on God for guidance every step of the way. In that short exercise, we were able to see how God's call made a way for Moses to reclaim shameful and rejected parts of himself. It gave us hope that we, too, could reclaim the disowned and shadowy parts of ourselves.

Signs of True Self

The phase of reclamation often begins with some signs that our true self has something to say to us. Depression and listlessness may be suggesting that we need to tend our inner life more carefully. If we can't shake some incident or interpretation of events that seems frozen, perhaps there is a secret asking for airtime. If we are especially critical or excessively concerned about time, perhaps our ego is trying to stay in control of something our soul is wanting. These are outward signs of inward distress, the signs of a divided self. They are signs that it's time to reclaim what we may have been ignoring, or even forgotten.

Marion Woodman, a Jungian analyst who has been a teacher and mentor for me, would say that these disowned parts become part of our shadow, unrecognized by the ego as part of our wholeness. In aging, Marion says, the soul wants union with these disowned parts. "The problem with the unconscious," she says, "is that it's not accessible to the conscious mind. You can't plan your way to soul union. You must look to your dreams and images released by body movement."

This is a time when some people seek help from a therapist or spiritual director. Others may find help in a dream group or a quilting circle. I decided to join a group of older women that met twice a year for a week in Marion's apartment. We would study a provocative Jungian text, work with a dream presented by one of the participants, and then adjourn to a nearby hall to do body work and paint or draw images evoked by the whole experience. I had been tracking my dreams for some time, but the addition of vocalizing and movement helped me feel the force of my dreams throughout my body, instead of just using my mind for analysis. Engaging the body, Marion suggests, is the essence of the quest for reclaiming the whole self. For me, the body movement followed by expressive art making was probably the most important addition to what I was already doing.

For three years during the period around the completion of my career, I set aside time each day to track my dreams as my inner world was stirred by these intensive experiences with Marion Woodman. One particularly vivid dream told me that my true self was in some danger:

> I am sitting in a theater, waiting for a play to begin. As the curtains open, two sisters come in from stage right, chattering happily with

market baskets on each arm. One remarks that it is time to get "her" out, and she opens a closet door. She pulls out a large black garbage bag and opens it. She lifts a crippled girl to a standing position and locks her leg braces in place. From my seat in the theater, I strongly identify with the crippled girl. The sisters leave.

In the second scene, the crippled girl is standing on a table, facing away from the audience, with her hands fully extended upward, over the scenery edge. Rain is pelting her hands, and she is making excited guttural sounds. I think to myself, "Oh, she's also mute." Just then, the sisters come back and begin tugging at her, trying to get her down off the table and back into the bag. I feel anxious and protective: "They'll cripple her for life if she falls and they lock those braces in place." I woke with a strong sense that I was being warned of some imminent danger.

When I shared this dream with my spiritual director, she noticed that I made reference to Helen Keller as I described the sounds that the crippled girl was making. She suggested that we hold the dream in prayerful silence together and that I pay attention to the message that was being tapped onto "my" hands by the rain. The word "come" arose almost immediately, and it stayed although I tried to make space for other possibilities. As we came out of the silence, I felt alive in every pore, as though I had touched a live wire. She suggested that I draw and dance the word "come" during the interval before our next meeting to see where it would lead.

My body reaction when I received the message from that rain was confirmation that it was time to follow that inner guidance to come home to myself, to give more attention to the "crippled girl" in my psyche. Did that mean I needed to give up my public teaching? Or did it mean that I needed to find some way to embrace some underdeveloped, mute, crippled part of myself to be a better teacher? Where could I go for more guidance? Who would be my Annie Sullivan?

Reclaiming the mute or crippled parts of ourselves can be a fearful journey or an adventure inward to uncover our neglected parts.

Dreams are not the only way to do that, but they provide a powerful source of guidance accessible to all if we can move past the cultural preference for logic, reason, and measurement. Another way to start the process of reclaiming these lost parts of our lives is to find a life coach or a spiritual director. Guides with training and experience in deep listening, who can suggest what to watch for, can help us move through this opaque period.

Creative aging is a process, not a race or a benchmark of enlightenment. In fact, in this part of the neutral zone we will probably feel lost, lonely, and small. If we can give ourselves permission to *not* know the next step, to stay in the womb of remembrance and let the natural process of gestation occur slowly, we are more likely to birth a whole and healthy inner core. Learning to pay attention and trust our inner wisdom for guidance about the next step underscores the words of Psalm 139: "I praise you, for I am fearfully and wonderfully made."

Body Speech

Some people are very aware of talents and interests they have set aside to fulfill their family responsibilities. Because they have traditionally been caretakers, women are more likely than men to have set aside personal dreams. Some of us have forgotten old interests and passions that need to be ignited again.

When Dana arrived in Washington, D.C., she was newly divorced and working as an event coordinator for a large company. Although she had always been attracted to movement and dance, she had never pursued it before, so I was surprised when she spoke excitedly about attending a national meeting of the Sacred Dance Guild for the first time. It was clear that she was fulfilling a long-held dream. Although she had moved to Washington to be near her grown children and grandchildren, she was ready to claim her independence, her singleness and authority as the author of her own life.

Dana applied for money from her church's Growing Edge Fund so that she could attend another meeting of the Sacred Dance Guild.

Along with this financial help, her support group helped her find an advocate, someone who was interested in helping Dana bring her experience back into the church community. Dana responded by gathering a group of dancers to lead body prayer in worship on special occasions. She hoped to start a dance group, but it didn't have enough collective energy to last. Still, she continued to invite others from the congregation to attend training events with her, and she held on to the hope that she could get a local group started.

When Dana qualified for Medicare, she retired from her corporate job and got involved in an expressive movement known as InterPlay. With a series of teachable forms, InterPlay helps people awaken to their body wisdom. It is neither scripted movement nor performance, but rather a connection with others through movement rather than words. As Dana progressed with this movement practice, she eventually entered the InterPlay leadership training program. I noticed that her body movements were becoming more fluid, more spontaneous. Almost single-handedly, she sponsored a monthly InterPlay experience at her church, and this time a group of regulars could be counted on to show up and participate. Soon the energy was flowing from InterPlay into worship and back out again. Others in the community entered the leadership training program, and finally after ten years of faithfully holding up her call to dance and movement, Dana has been successful in her efforts as a volunteer to establish a Washington, D.C., chapter of InterPlayers.

Dana's divorce had left her identity stranded. As she reclaimed her interest in dance and movement, her involvement with InterPlay gave her a place to use her organizational and administrative skills. Because she had been willing to offer her undeveloped desire for movement in the rich soil of her church community, the seed of her interest put down strong roots. That does not always happen, of course. Without the proper soil and water, no seed will sprout. Reclamation is never a guarantee of future growth, but it is always the kernel of possibility.

Listening Community

Having others who are not invested in the outcome listen to us can help us reclaim our lost parts. Often a spouse is too close or the patterns are already set in a family, and there is not much reason to change unless a crisis upsets the pattern. But having a community that can help us listen for inner guidance can be a positive environment for creative aging.

Richard has been an environmental lawyer for the federal government. He was raised Catholic, but had been away from church for many years. He had joined a local Buddhist *sangha* and found that meditation with others began to open up his inner life. Then he joined a church, looking for some way to reclaim his Christian tradition if he could. After attending worship for several Sundays, he signed up for a class. And then another. Nobody demanded his allegiance to a creed or a body of beliefs, and he began to feel more comfortable.

Finally, Richard decided he was ready to join a mission group—one that sponsored adult education. Within the context of the group, Richard was able to name his doubts about continuing to work as a lawyer in the field of environmental protection and to name his desire for other work. With the help of weekly written reports to his spiritual guide and some directed reading, Richard finally asked for a Quaker "clearness committee," during which several people asked him prayerful questions, trusting that Richard's inner wisdom would guide his responses and clarify what his soul was longing for. At the conclusion, he felt led to take a long sabbatical, and he began to let his clients know that he would not be available for new work.

It turned out that one of Richard's hopes, when he entered environmental law, had been to do international work. And just as he decided to set his vocation as an environmental attorney aside, an invitation came for an environmental conference in China. With excitement, he said yes to that opportunity, knowing it might be the path of more generative work within his own field.

Having a listening community with no agenda about what he "ought" to do was an important step for Richard. My experience tells me that if we have a committed group of listeners, people who can ask the kind of thoughtful "queries" that Quakers do, we will be able to bring a more holistic awareness to bear on the questions we have about what to do with our time and energy. There may be times when we need the one-on-one help of a therapist, when the questions that come up are too big for a group of caring adults to hold. But if we understand that this process is a natural one, and that feelings of dis-ease or depression are normal as we make the inner transition from a full-time career to something that is different and more soulful, we can rely on friends who are committed to the same intentional journey. The spiritual practice of finding or creating a listening community is a part of reclaiming our true selves.

Buried Gifts

There is a parable in scripture about using our talents. On the surface, the story seems to suggest that we need to "use it or lose it." A wealthy landowner gave one man ten talents, another five, and another one. The first two managed to double their money through some shrewd investments, and the owner was pleased to reward them when he returned. But the third man was frightened of the master's expectations, so he buried his talent in the ground for safe-keeping.

Something in us resonates with this fearful servant, the one who buried his talent. Is it because we know there are gifts we have been given that we've buried or ignored? Do we also sense that it will take some real courage to uncover the treasure that we have buried? Are we afraid of what we will find if we dig up those buried talents? Or do we simply pity the poor man who is overcome by his fears?

Most of us have buried parts of ourselves that we felt would not survive in the competitive marketplace. Most often, the first casualties are gifts of wonder and slowness, of playfulness and caring.

Sometimes we bury gifts of beauty, music, or theater, or personality traits, such as a sense of humor or the ability to listen, that seem to have no commercial value, so we judge them to be less worthy. If we have cultivated them at all, it's probably been during small breaks between larger responsibilities. Or we might have kept them stowed away, waiting for a time when it would seem right to dig them up again.

For Steve, a major heart attack was the catalyst for digging up his hidden treasure—his love for gardening. As an orthopedic surgeon, he had come a long way from the farm where he grew up. He had built a successful practice and enjoyed the perks that came with it. But by the time he reached midlife, Steve was working too hard and drinking too much, until his heart gave out. Fortunately, Steve recognized the warning. As part of his twelve-step recovery, Steve remembered how much he had loved gardening with his mother when he was a child. Each year after his heart attack, Steve's garden grew bigger and his health improved. Although he continued to practice medicine into his seventies, he had found a new balance between the exacting skill of surgery and hard physical labor outdoors. Every summer, the harvest table at his church was filled with extra produce from his garden. Steve recovered a source of gladness and generosity that was buried in his childhood until the time was right for it to emerge again.

Reclamation doesn't happen overnight. It is a process of drawing energy from the past, discovering forgotten loves, and exploring deeply buried veins of precious resources that have been ignored or repressed. Digging up gifts from the past requires space and time for musing, for following intuitions and feelings to uncover yearnings that have stayed mute in the background. In the midst of a busy career, we seldom have or take the time for this kind of exploration. For Steve, the twelve-step process began to open his inner world. It gave him a clear process for examining his motives and dealing with old issues, and it encouraged doing more of what he loved as a child as a healing practice.

Serial Exploration

Reclamation can also be a process of intentional experimentation and elimination. David's story is a classic example. He graduated from college with a degree in electrical engineering and went to work for IBM. He began a steady career climb and eventually became one of their Golden Circle managers. Soon after he turned fifty, David began to study tai chi as a stress management technique. He approached the forms of tai chi with dedication and thoroughness, mastering each level until he could teach them. Meanwhile, his division of IBM was acquired by another and then another company, and his satisfaction at work began to decline. At sixty, he took an early retirement opportunity and began very methodically to examine his other interests for something that would provide both structure and satisfaction.

David had a desire to deepen his spiritual life, and he decided that he would offer a class at his synagogue. He wanted to form a spirituality group that would explore some of the spiritual issues around aging. He discussed it with the rabbi and then offered his leadership. After three years of trying to move the group toward deeper and more personal topics, he decided that this was not the learning community he needed to share his passion for life, and he stepped back from teaching.

David is also a voracious reader, so he thought that volunteering at the central library might be a possibility. But he quickly found that they were not organized to use volunteer help. He would show up and find that there was nobody to answer his questions or provide direction. Although the library option was not the answer David was looking for, with each attempt at reclaiming his passion, he was becoming more clear about what his mind and heart needed at this stage of life.

Finally, David found that another longtime interest, American folklore, was the right place for his encore years. He already had an extensive collection of music and had made it a point to develop relationships with many local performers. He took the next step and began volunteering at the American Folklife Center at the Library of Congress two days a week. Once they realized his level of knowledge, the director gave David a significant project of his own. She trusted him with sorting and creating a filing system for a valuable collection of materials. That fed his desire to learn and grow along with giving his time. Over the past decade, David has become a valuable member of the center's research team, as well as a regular participant in the other activities sponsored by the folklife center. David found new focus in this lifelong interest and is making a valuable contribution to a field far from where he spent his professional career.

Pain and Suffering

Although it would be easier to avoid the role of suffering and loss in reclaiming parts of our true selves, we all know—and probably dread—that particular pathway. We live in a culture that implies technology can protect us from emotional pain and that money can buy security, but we also know that love will always draw us into the greater rhythms of death and new life. In this winter season for the soul, endings sometimes mean reclaiming life from the ashes of an actual death.

Abbie was happily moving into the generative period of her life when her only son committed suicide. He had long struggled with depression, but he had seemed to be moving into adulthood successfully when Abbie and her husband got the word that he had taken an overdose of pills. Abbie was devastated, but her church community gathered to celebrate his life and to comfort the family. Then the hard work of reclamation began. Abbie and her husband joined a grief group of other parents who had suffered similar tragedies. They listened to each other, asked gentle questions, and grieved together. After several months, they found that they were able to meet with newly bereaved parents to offer support.

Abbie's creativity finally gave her a way to live with their loss and reclaim a part of herself. She had been a professional writer before her marriage and had kept a journal all through the years of raising her family. When she had gone to work, she had taught special education classes, but writing poetry had always been her avocation. After she retired, she joined a poetry group and began submitting her work to literary journals. "I've been turned down by all the best magazines," she laughs ruefully, "but I just keep writing. It's my therapy."

Although it is important not to romanticize pain or loss, a new call can sometimes arise out of suffering—our own or our response to someone else's pain. Reclaiming the parts of ourselves that we have denied or set aside to be "successful" in the eyes of the world can indeed open our hearts to the reality of pain and suffering. When we allow that to happen, we become more fully human, more integrated as our true selves, capable of deep connection with the needs of others.

Reclaiming gifts from the past is particularly important for the generative work ahead. Beyond the obvious assistance of a therapist or spiritual director, there are many ways of doing this healing work of reclamation. As we wander around in the neutral zone between career and creative aging, we may pick up interests that were set aside while we earned a living or raised a family, as Dana did with InterPlay. Steve reconnected with his background on a farm through the twelve-step program and recovered his old interest in gardening. And methodical experimentation provided David with a way to turn an old interest into a volunteer job with real consequences for a field that had fed his soul for many years.

Having a listening community provided the help that Richard needed to make space in his career for a sabbatical, to reexamine his focus and pursue an interest in international policy on the environment. For Abbie, a grief group and then a poetry group provided her with a way through personal tragedy and helped her reclaim an interest in writing, which has become more important in her aging. Both found the help of others essential.

This particular phase of the third round of call seems to need the presence of others to help us unearth hidden gifts that we buried in the past and bring them forward in a more conscious and intentional way.

Spiritual Practice: Dreams

During the deep winter period of reclaiming neglected passions from the past, tracking your dreams and doing something with them can be especially helpful.

Tracking your dreams doesn't have to be complicated or analytical. Giving them some visible form seems to be enough to encourage this inner source of wisdom. I keep a small package of crayons and my dream notebook in the bathroom and make a quick smudgy picture to catch the main action by the dim glow of the nightlight. The next morning, I fill in details with words and simply let those images become part of my sense of direction.

Keeping your dreams in a special notebook is a way of bringing these images into your consciousness, giving them some objective reality, and treating them with respect. It doesn't take long to realize that these images come from beyond your conscious mind, because who would make these crazy connections? Sharing your dreams with a therapist or spiritual director can help you bring into consciousness the vitality hidden in your dreams.

A dream group with someone who can tend those dreams without quick analysis can also bring a sense of Sabbath to this period of reclamation. Being in a dream group might also give you support for adding body movement to that inner search. Movement can be a powerful way to bring your whole self into the picture, but it's hard to initiate on your own.

A coach or spiritual director might offer the privacy and focus needed to begin naming your hunches or intuitions about a new direction. A church or spiritual group might also be a place to find kindred seekers. I have also noticed that art classes can become an informal community where people find support for reclaiming some neglected interest.

Questions to Ponder

1. Is there some way you could pay more attention to your dreams? Find someone to share them with? Give them objective reality with color or clay?

2. Do you have a small group of listeners in your life? Are there two or three others who might offer thoughtful questions in the manner of a Quaker clearness committee?

3. Are you aware of old interests, such as gardening or paper dolls, that might hold the seed of a new direction?

4. If you are a more systematic thinker, what interests or hobbies might you explore?

5. What has sustained you through difficult times? Is that something you might develop?

5

REVELATION
Where Does Newness Come From?

> I taught you to be more comfortable with your
> uncertainty. This acceptance of ambiguity will lead
> you to ... a mystery-driven life.
> —James Hollis, *What Matters Most*

In late winter, when days begin to lengthen but the danger of
frost is still there, how do acorns know to begin sprouting?
Where does newness come from? What inspires creativity? What
prompts playfulness? Imagination? How does the future enter
into the present moment? These are the questions that arise in the
latter half of the neutral zone of transition, when we are still not
sure what form our generativity will take but sense that the climate has shifted. Hope begins to put out tiny tendrils, testing for
warmth and light.

If reclamation involves looking back to pick up scattered parts of
our lives and draw them together again, then revelation means
looking ahead for new and unexpected glimpses of grace.

Just as the axis of our spinning planet begins to tip toward spring,
so, too, some gyroscope in us begins to lean toward the future,
moving us toward hope and possibility. I don't think we can *make*
this happen or hurry the process, but there is something in the
human spirit that reaches toward light, revealing our interconnec-
tions with unknown parts of creation.

As we breathe in the spaciousness of the new terrain that comes with aging, and breathe out the tightness that we have carried in our bodies for so long to meet the demands of constant accessibility, the strict lines of focus and schedule begin to soften. Without the pressure to produce tangible results, day after day after day, our inner world expands. We can begin to engage our souls in a conversation with greater themes, find that greater forces are at work. Old identities may dissolve and new ones form to fit who we are becoming.

We do not have to understand nature's impulse toward growth to observe that it happens. We do not have to believe in the God of our fathers and mothers to accept the reality of a spiritual realm beyond what we can count and measure. What person hasn't stood close to the ocean or paused on a mountaintop, awestruck by the carved beauty of stone and sky, instantly aware that we are part of some greater unfolding drama? What person hasn't experienced the surprise of being at exactly the right place at the right time?

Revelation is a momentary glimpse of the bigger picture, pointing to a source beyond ourselves. No matter which religious tradition has given us language for our spiritual lives, nature reminds us that we are not in charge. The natural world has its own fierce edge, where death and resurrection occur without our aid or consent. Creativity and newness is a constant if only we have eyes to see. Our human capacity to deny or distance ourselves from this reality is a peculiar gift, but one we must wrestle with if we are to move from stagnation into generativity. Because we have the mental capacity to deaden ourselves to the wonder around us, we also have the power to embrace the mysterious pulse of creative energy that is flowing through us.

Gordon Cosby, a founder of Church of the Saviour in Washington, D.C., has been one of my spiritual guides over the years, and listening to recordings of his sermons has nourished many a long commute. One stands out as I think of revelation and generativity: "Called to Be Creative." In it, Gordon proposes, "If you are not creative in the peculiar way that you are destined to be creative, you will be angry—deeply frustrated and angry."

Gordon goes on to say that "creativity is a function of the inner imagination.... Creativity comes when we are in contact with the living contents of the inner world, the 'inner fish,' and bring them to the surface and give them expression in our lives." How easily Gordon spoke those words—"the living contents of the inner world"—as though anyone could cast a net and find such a school of inner fish. And yet this was exactly what he meant: this inner realm is accessible to anyone. For Gordon, the source of newness was not limited or rare, did not require special talent or education, but was available to anyone who would pay attention to her inner life through listening prayer, silence, dream work, and other spiritual disciplines. Revelation and creativity swim together under the surface of our lives.

When I picture this "inner fish," I imagine it moving noiselessly in the underwater depths of our dreams and imagination. I recall the biblical stories where crowds were fed with five loaves and two fish, miraculous food so abundant that overflowing baskets were collected afterward. I remember how Jesus called to his discouraged disciples after they had fished fruitlessly all night, saying, "Throw your nets on the other side." And when they did, the nets were filled to bursting.

When our nets are empty after much effort and patient fishing for inspiration, we may need to cast our nets on the other side and troll for the hidden fish swimming below the obvious events of our lives. The questions for us at this stage of life are: "Where is the other side toward which we should throw our nets? What are the inner fish swimming below the surface of our lives? Where are we hearing our call?"

Synchronicity

As much as we would like quick or ready answers to these questions, revelation is not a one-time event. Sometimes it comes to the surface over a period of time, through a series of events that begin to catch our attention. Simultaneous events occur with no causal connection, but the timing is startling. Things seem to "come together" in a miraculous way: a woman dreams of confronting her boss and the next day, it happens; a phone call comes at just the right moment; a letter arrives with the answer to a question you have not asked aloud. Jung defined this kind of synchronicity as the meaningful connection between two events, one inner and psychic and the other outer and physical. Such "coincidences" suggest an underlying pattern to all existence that goes beyond the observable pattern of cause and effect. Synchronicity is a signal that we are participating in a greater story of creation that is quite different from the usual chain of events.

Gordon Cosby tells a touching story of Abraham Lincoln, who had a sense of his destiny as a leader along with the reality of his limited opportunities for education in rural Illinois. One day, a stranger came to his door and offered Lincoln the contents of a barrel for one dollar. Lincoln, who did not have the money to spare, sensed that he should give the man the money. Sometime later, he discovered that the barrel contained a complete edition of English judge William Blackstone's *Commentaries on the Laws of England,* which allowed Lincoln to get the education he needed to read for the bar and become a lawyer. In this sermon on creativity, Gordon spoke of the seeming lack of connection between these two streams: Lincoln's call to be a leader and the arrival of this barrel. Such synchronicity is an example of revelation and guidance from beyond our human experience. To be open to such events is, in itself, a creative act.

When Martin Luther King Jr. spelled out his dream of equal opportunity for all Americans, black and white, segregation was still rampant. There was no evidence that such a dream could be realized any time soon. But as King's vision was striking a chord of hope in many people, television was also making the injustice he railed against more visible. Although television did not cause the civil rights movement, it is likely that widespread acts of civil disobedience would not have resulted in ending segregation without that media coverage. The synchronous timing of King's leadership and the advent of television brought about a new level of freedom and diversity in America that we can see today.

In another more personal example, Kathryn, a tenured faculty member at a local university, realized after a recent faculty retreat that the grant she needed to fund a program she had been promoting for many years would never get written. Usually a hopeful person, she felt desperate this time. Though she was just two years from retirement, she felt weary and discouraged, unsure whether she could physically carry her teaching load and worried about creating enough income to live on once she retired. She also has an adult son with a severe mental disease who lives with her, and an adopted daughter, who is a single parent with three small children, lives nearby. She helps them both just to survive. All that was bearing down on her after the faculty retreat. Even though tenure assured her job security, she felt that her job was at risk.

Kathryn decided to cast her net on the other side, and she began to offer clinical supervision to Latina social workers at a federally funded center, not at the university. She also found a small church that welcomed her three grandchildren every Sunday, so she was able to offer her daughter a weekly respite by keeping the children every Saturday night and bringing them with her to church the following morning. The church, in turn, helped her to trust her inner life—her prayers, dreams, and imaginings.

With her fears and hopes in a fierce inner wrestling match, Kathryn had a dream. In it, she was telling her department chair about her despair and asking for help. She decided that the dream signaled alignment between her inner soul and her outer situation, so she made an appointment to see her supervisor. When I next saw Kathryn, she was beaming. The supervisor was willing and able to help with other options, and it has unleashed a wave of creativity in her both at home and at work. Kathryn is trusting her inner wisdom to move in the direction she wants to go after retirement and is taking steps in that direction, whether or not the university is able to support it. The synchronicity of her dream and the unexpected reality of her supervisor's reaction got Kathryn's attention.

Old Sorrows

Revelation can also occur when an old sorrow or an old wound points the way to action instead of defeat. A child with Down's syndrome prompts a mother to join others to found a L'Arche home that will offer humane care for her disabled son. Having a deaf mother encourages Alexander Graham Bell to develop new listening devices. Divorce and the threat of destitution sparks formation of OWL, the Older Women's League. Instead of grieving helplessly, those who see a tragedy as a possible call can move from the mystical realm into practical results. Like a curtain swinging open to reveal the future, a small step toward changing the situation can lead to something much larger.

Eunice Kennedy Shriver, founder of the Special Olympics, traced her passion for better treatment of the developmentally disabled back to her sister, Rosemary, who was "warehoused" in an asylum for many years and did not get the kind of support that Eunice dreamed of. While the Kennedy brothers pursued a path of public service through politics, Eunice found a call to help the handicapped, which grew out of a simple desire to share the joy of competitive sports with those who were left out of most school programs. The resulting Special Olympics program began with a magazine article she wrote for the *Saturday Evening Post* in 1962, just after her brother, John, became president. Today, more than 2.5 million athletes in one hundred and eighty countries take part in Special Olympics. Her son, Timothy, is currently the president and CEO of Special Olympics, and all five of her children are involved in some form of public service. From the old sorrow of a family secret came a whole generation of service. Although we know there is much more to the story of Kennedy family service, this example of how an old sorrow was transformed into action strikes me as a revelation. Eunice Shriver could have been satisfied with her role as a superhostess, but she felt called to a larger purpose.

On a smaller scale, sometimes the future comes toward us when a partner or spouse is touched by illness or disability. It is not the future we planned, but it is the reality we are given. How we react to that situation will be our choice, our destiny. If we can find meaning and purpose in surrendering to the demands of caring for that disabled partner, we can understand this period as a unique calling. If we think it is a cruel cosmic joke, we may simply leave. The difference is our response to what is being revealed.

Barriers, blocks, and obstacles are an inevitable part of life. In responding to the wounds of others, as Shriver did, our creativity can also be unleashed to face the disappointments of life. If we constantly look for the easiest path, the one with no opposition, or to false leads, we may limit our creativity, waiting to pour through us into the physical world. If we are willing to cast our nets on the other side of the boat, into the unknown waters where creativity swims just out of sight in the unconscious realm, newness awaits.

Spotting Gifts

Sometimes revelation comes indirectly, not from within but from what we discover about ourselves in other people. Sometimes we catch sight of our hidden strengths when we see them reflected in someone else. As adults, we tend to be known for what we already do. It is not likely that someone is going to tell us about our emerging gifts. But we may notice a feeling of envy or wistfulness, which can be a clue that someone is carrying a gift that is asking to be born in ourselves. If we take the time to examine our feelings, we can sometimes identify a gift that is asking for recognition in our own lives.

Other people often tell me that my husband, Peter, is "the engineer" and I am "the artist." He and I both know that he has a strong artistic bent (he has made woodblocks to print Christmas cards and taken a sculptural crochet class at the Smithsonian), but our friends tend to see his technical skills first. Peter is a dutiful Eagle Scout by nature and often sets aside his creative gifts to meet the needs of others. His spiritual director, though, sees his artistic side and once gave him a nicely lettered sign that is now posted over his desk: "Get thee to thy studio."

For Peter's sixtieth birthday, we shopped for a new camera together, and I was delighted that he chose something more expensive than he would have bought just for himself. With the new camera, Peter began taking pictures of the retreat farm where we often go, and he turned those images into cards, selling them at the church bookstore and giving the proceeds to the retreat center. The more positive feedback Peter got from other people, the better he got with his photography and printing process. He began to think of himself as an artist. Meanwhile, I practically stopped taking pictures in an effort to leave that field open to Peter.

Then a revelation occurred. When Peter's camera rolled out of his pack on the airplane coming home from Guatemala, we were very distressed because we thought we'd lost all our pictures. I had taken a few with my old camera, and I assumed they would not be good because I wasn't being careful. However, we discovered I had taken about two hundred pictures, and when we looked at them, we were stunned by their quality. It was not only a fairly complete narrative of the trip, but also we could see that my eye had been keen. My unconscious artist had been busy with the camera while my conscious mind was busy tying rebar and pouring cement. The accidental loss of Peter's camera invited the photographer in me to step forth again.

I had unwittingly been measuring the distribution of artistry, subtracting my supply as Peter increased his. This kind of hidden equation is an old story, developed in childhood: more for him means less for me. As adults, we may be operating with that same mentality when it no longer pertains. Sometimes it takes an accident, such as losing a camera, to claim our hidden gifts.

Sometimes we may discover a hidden gift by volunteering to do something we haven't done before. Whatever impulse prompts us to offer can be seen as a sprout of creativity, a seed ready to open. At that vulnerable point, we may be surprised and encouraged by the positive reaction of others. Muriel had purchased a small lot on which she hoped to build a "universal design" house, with full handicapped accessibility, in which she could live out her later years. Her brother, Gene, offered to draw up some plans for her "dream house."

Before this, Muriel had had no idea that he had any skills in that area; she had never seen or known about this talent before. She was amazed at how good he was at it. He had obviously observed her values and desires and had included many of the subtle preferences she hadn't expressly stated. Thrilled, she exclaimed, "I didn't know you could do that!" Even though his exploration of this gift may have been tentative, her reaction and reinforcement were part of confirming this buried talent.

In the latter part of the neutral zone, in this late winter season, finding people who can offer warmth, light, and encouragement is particularly important as we seek to discover our call. If we sense that we are at the stage of wanting to offer something of ourselves to others, it will be important to put ourselves in a position where we can be with people who will give us these kinds of encouraging reactions.

The Long View

Sometimes focusing our vision for the future is an unfolding revelation. Will's experience as a teacher in Ethiopia with the Peace Corps planted seeds that were cultivated on the side during his primary career as a lawyer. Will had grown up with a deep commitment to helping the poor and marginalized, particularly children, and in his work at Children's National Medical Center in Washington, D.C., he handled court cases on behalf of abused and neglected children. Later, he worked for the U.S. Department of Defense in child protective services. Yet, by his own account, his policy work was becoming farther and farther removed from the children and families he was trying to help.

As Will approached the point where he could take early retirement, his work felt more and more bureaucratic. Adversarial politics dominated the discussion, and the idea of winning cases had lost its appeal. "I feel sapped and depressed much of the time," he reported, wondering what he would do in the next stage of his life.

Throughout his career, Will had always enjoyed teaching biblical studies and thinking about theology. Because he was in a church where his gifts for teaching were welcomed, and offering courses had provided him with an ongoing framework for study and teaching, he felt that one option would be to attend seminary and become a student again. Another would be to find a place where he could do more teaching and be paid for it.

In addition, Will knew he would love to be a grandfather, but because his daughters were both single and showed no signs of wanting children, that did not seem like an immediate prospect. So Will and his wife decided to mentor a boy whose mother had just been released from jail. They take him swimming and recently committed to getting the boy to soccer practice because his mother does not have a car. It is clear that direct involvement with one needy child is feeding something in Will's soul. For now, he's letting these two possibilities, teaching and mentoring, develop toward something more tangible and specific.

Taking a long view of interests and emotional impact is a form of revelation. It comes gradually, often slower than we would like. If certain themes recur, such as Will's dissatisfaction with bureaucratic negotiation and his enjoyment of direct involvement, it can illuminate the next few steps on a longer path. It is important to give slow revelations plenty of time to unfold and not make snap judgments about the next step.

Resonance

Observing changes in what we are interested in can also be a source of insight about the marginalized parts of our souls that may be asking for more attention as we age. I spoke with a therapist who is following a thread of resonance between herself and a Holocaust survivor who has some signs of dementia. Karen feels a sense of urgency to discover why this particular woman was able to live with such resilience and hopefulness following her traumatic wartime experience in which she was the only survivor in her family. Karen spoke ardently of her admiration for this Holocaust survivor and told me she wanted to write this woman's story as a book for teens, although she had never written for publication before.

As we talked, Karen discovered a similarity between the survivor's story and her own teenage experience of belonging to a gang. Karen had felt trapped by her peers and forced to abide by gang rules, completely without protection from her parents or other adults. She, too, was a survivor. She discovered that she wanted to claim her own story of hopefulness and survival.

Once Karen moved into the terrain of her story, she also stumbled over the strong messages of fear and incompetence. Her real fear was that she couldn't write with enough skill and grace to honor her client's story—or her own. Although she has a good reputation as a therapist for teens in the field of addictions, she is now ready to address some of the demons in her own past. We talked about how she might deflate those inner critics by writing this woman's story, and then, in time, she might be ready to write her own. The resonance between Karen's story and another woman's Holocaust experience provided a heartbeat of hopefulness in an otherwise unexplored inner terrain.

Revelation can also happen when our individual desire resonates with a movement that is picking up steam in the wider culture. I think of the small recycling center on the island off the coast of Maine where Peter and I go as volunteer pastors. Five years ago, the island was struggling with trash: car hulks, washing machines, bottles, insulation, paint cans, Styrofoam, and plastic jugs. Years of accumulated junk filled backyards and ditches. Some people did their best to take their trash with them when they left, but year-round residents despaired about the cooperation that would be needed to turn the tide and clean up the island.

On the mainland, recycling was just getting started, and one of the recycling centers agreed to take a truckload of large objects made of metal. This was a good place to start. After talking to a couple of key people, the island baker decided she would just rent a truck, bring it out on the ferry, and return after a one-hour pickup with what could be loaded in that time. She put up notices that large items could be picked up if people were willing to call and get on a pickup list. Smaller items could be deposited on the parsonage lawn, where we were living at the time. A builder with a summer place on the island came with his Bobcat to lift the heaviest stuff, and we all cheered when the truck pulled away, completely full, in time to catch the ferry back.

The following year, people on the island built a recycling center with several small sheds and staffed it on Saturdays so people could bring separated trash. T-shirts spread the word about the recycling effort. Signs sprouted: "No dumping! We will track you down!" Each year was a milestone, and the island began to look like people cared—because most of us did. On the beach, an artist playfully grouped plastic trash and plastic rope by color and made "crap circles," which Peter photographed and turned into cards for sale to support emergency medical care on the island.

That's how revelation comes to a community. When one person in a key position has a vision, invites volunteer support, and simply starts, there is no telling where it will grow. This kind of resonance is like two tuning forks, each mounted on a sound box to amplify its vibrations. When one tuning fork is struck with a mallet, the second will begin vibrating even though it has not been directly struck. In the same way, one person's story may set up a sympathetic vibration in someone else, and one person's vision may set up a sympathetic vibration in the wider community.

☙❧

In the end, vision comes from knowing what we want. At this stage of life, we don't have to wait for someone else to approve. Robert Fritz, founder of Technologies for Creating, in his book *The Path of Least Resistance*, writes that the way to get the vision of what we truly want is to *make it up*. That is the beginning of any creative act—to imagine the future we want. If we have nurtured our passions in the reclamation phase and learned to trust our creativity in this revelation phase, we can tend the inner spring of newness.

Revelation happens each time insight expands our vision forward. Acting on our dreams takes a sense of right timing, which is another form of synchronicity. Grace happens. The right person appears.

Hope rises and wonder returns as a possibility. Synchronicity suggests a source beyond the here and now. We feel miraculously restored and ready to move.

When we open our eyes to something that has been building around us for a long time—an old sorrow or a constant irritant such as trash on an island—we may feel called to take action. Some people take action easily because they have done it all their lives. Others are ready to volunteer if somebody else takes the lead. When we're ready, crossing the barrier between thought and action is the next step in claiming the creative journey we are on.

Spiritual Practice: Writing

Writing for a given amount of time each day can gradually move you beyond performance into the realm of free association. Writing freely will help you express those hidden currents of soul fish swimming beneath the waves of compare, contrast, and critique that most of us retain from classroom assignments or exams. Although I prefer to do this kind of writing by hand, some people are freed by using a computer.

Writing daily can reveal glimpses of what your future might hold and expand your vision. Writing is a way to see what is churning around inside. It can help you uncover what you are longing for beneath your busyness. It is a good way to track feelings and notice synchronicities, a way to "cast your net on the other side" and discover inner resources you were not aware of. Pay special attention to recurrent irritants. They may be the nagging sign of a new call. Rather than blaming someone else for those feelings, the first step is to notice them. The second is to ask what your feelings reveal. Is there something asking for attention? Could that be a seed of call?

In the age of Twitter and tweets, writing for the purpose of knowing ourselves seems, on the surface, to be a dying art. But I have noticed a surprising interest in writing as a spiritual practice among the people I meet on retreats. People respond readily to writing prompts ("I've always dreamed of doing …" or "If I had a month to live, I would …"), and they are usually grateful for a chance to read them aloud in a sympathetic group. There is something about reading aloud that might allow you to hear what you are saying in a different way.

Start with a simple spiral notebook, pose a question at the top of the left-hand page, and fill both facing pages before you stop. Here are some prompts you might use:

- Questions about my work now are …
- Something I've always dreamed of doing …
- What I love to do with my hands …
- If I had a free day, I would …
- What I would hate to give up …

Questions to Ponder

1. It's easy to identify the things that make us angry or disgusted. It's harder to identify what we want to support or stand for. Look at the daily newspaper and circle one or two articles that really tug at your heart. What would you like to change? What do you dream of?

2. Have you ever experienced a sense of being at exactly the right place at the right time? Have you experienced synchronicity, when two unrelated events coincide perfectly? What might this be telling you?

3. Think back to your family, faith tradition, or social context, or a glaring example of injustice that tugs at your heart. Is there an old sorrow that fuels your passion today? Is there an early experience you might want to heal by writing it as a story?

4. Can you think of an example of resonance between yourself and another person's story? Or between a desire for your family (community, school, church) and their responsiveness?

6

CROSSING POINT
Joining Inner and Outer Worlds

Neither the hair shirt nor the soft berth will do.
The place God calls you to is the place where
your deep gladness and the world's deep hunger meet.
—**Frederick Buechner,** *Wishful Thinking*

Until this point, the phases of transition are almost entirely internal. Making the decision to embrace a new identity, a new calling, is like crossing a turbulent river and marks a major passage from feelings of stagnation and inaction to making practical assessments that will result in generativity. It takes courage and clear purpose. It requires that we leave some things behind—old habits, old fears, even old friends—as we make the passage to a new form of work. A call that has been forming slowly is now ready to take shape in the world. It is time to wake up, to claim the warmth and sunshine of spring.

The crossing point between pondering and productive work brings us to the point of visible new beginnings. At first, questions swirl like whitewater over rapids. How do we know when it's time to act, to move, to translate revelation into action, impulse into motion? What prompts us to step into swirling waters of change and strike out for the other side with a firm resolve?

With all the choices we have, how can we say a firm yes—especially when we know it will mean other noes? How much can we trust our inner wisdom? Claim our own authority? Can we see our connection with the rest of creation? Do we believe that our lives have a larger purpose than just passing the time with a minimum of discomfort before we die?

These are the questions that face us as our call to "What's next?" begins to take shape, as we move from internal ideas about a new work into the outer world of action. To cross the boundary into this new territory, we need to let go of our fears and claim what we have seen in our dreams, what we have experienced in our bodies, what we have felt in our hearts. Instead of propping up an old image of who we once were, it's time to drop our pretensions and plan the next steps toward what we believe in.

In his description of the path that leads to generativity, Robert Fritz, author of *The Path of Least Resistance,* says we first need a clear vision, which I think is akin to revelation, of what we want to create. It is not enough to know what we do *not* want. Problem solving is not creative, nor is avoiding what we don't want. That may be a hint, a clue to shaping our future, but reaction is not enough to unleash the positive force of our lives.

Knowing what we *do* want is essential. If we spend our time criticizing or complaining about what we don't like, our desired outcome will never happen. Our call is a deep desire, something that may have been with us from a very young age. It's the clear purpose that grows out of reclaiming the past and embracing the future. It is, as author and theologian Frederick Buechner puts it, "the place where your deep gladness and the world's deep hunger meet." Now is the time to embrace it. Now is the time to pay attention to your soul speech rather than what other people expect. You can become the author of your life by becoming the change you want.

Sometimes an anniversary, such as a high school reunion or a significant birthday, sparks evaluation. This can bring us to the next step on the creative path, which Fritz describes as recognizing the reality of where we are and letting ourselves know the limits and needs of our situation. Facing these realities means making an honest assessment of what we actually have to work with: health, wealth, loves, and longings. As we look at these practical matters, there are two old ghosts that will surely arise: fear and lethargy. These feelings can haunt our calculations, pushing us back toward the neutral zone of wishing and dreaming or criticism rather than forging ahead into action. Our culture encourages both as a substitute for making a new start at this stage of life. Long-term fears about health care can overwhelm plans for adventure and excitement. And sheer laziness can dampen our dreams for a better world.

This brings us to the point of figuring out how to work with the tension between what we want and the reality of where we are. Holding that tension takes work. The goal is not to get *rid* of the tension but to *live* with it and use its energy to move forward. If we can remember that discomfort is always part of creating new things, we can develop more flexibility at this stage.

This crossing point is a critical time, but there are helpers available and choices to make. There are coaches, counselors, volunteer centers, churches, and educational institutions where we can get help in defining our gifts, experience, skills, and interests. We do not have to do that work alone. Sometimes the stimulation of a class can open doors and give us the boost we need to move ahead. Being with a career-transition group can also help us dig deeper and find the relevant decisions and actions we might be willing to do on our own. Finding a coach is another way to make this crossing between inner promptings and outward action. Articulating ideas and sharing them with others is a way of moving vague hopes into conscious planning.

Assessing Needs

At this point in the cycle of generative call, we may need to revisit the question of our real needs for work and rest, for money and recognition, for health care and stimulation. Writing things down can be a good bridge from factual data to understanding that information in a new way. Tracking our actual expenditures for a year, for example, can be a very revealing exercise but one that is surprisingly hard to do. We may discover places where we're spending huge sums without much to show for it. When I decided to undertake this simple task of recording all my daily expenditures, I discovered that I had gotten into the habit of stopping for a skim latte nearly every day. I was shocked to see that I was spending more than a thousand dollars in a year without even thinking about it. It's now easier to have my latte at home and save the store-bought one for a special occasion with a friend.

A realistic assessment of our financial needs and wants, and how we want to use whatever means we have, can give us more freedom to move, to engage in a different kind of work that takes us to the edge of risk and excitement rather than surrounding ourselves with comfort and security. When my dad, who had been a family physician all his adult life, closed his medical office, doctors then were not covered by Social Security, and although he had saved and invested carefully, his main assets were a paid-off house and a small holly farm. He needed income, but he had calculated expenses and saved enough to give himself a year to find a new way to offer his many years of practical experience.

My dad had a sense that he wanted to work for an organization that would carry malpractice insurance for him, but he did not have a clear picture. In that sabbatical year, he tried emergency room service but found it too pressured. He explored the Peace Corps and Presbyterian mission work, but neither of those worked out. Finally, he applied for a short-term assignment through the Bureau of Indian Affairs and discovered that it was the right combination of challenge and financial support. With its three- to six-month assignments, it allowed him time to come home between assignments to integrate the experience and tend to the cuttings that were growing in the greenhouse on the holly farm.

Assessing needs includes such unplanned realities as changes in the stock market and pension fund failures. Many people are now facing the reality that they can't retire because of stock losses, mortgage trouble, or other economic woes. At sixty or sixty-five, more people are finding that they have to work longer than they had planned, or have to go out and get a job because of necessity rather than desire. Sometimes an economic need can be a spur to new experience. I know of a sheltered, middle-class mother who went to work for the U.S. Postal Service at age fifty-seven to get health care for her son—and learned of a whole new world among her coworkers.

The economic changes in recent years have caused huge shifts in expectations. If we have lived with the image of leisure and travel as the reward for years of hard work, the economic necessity for working longer will be a burden and not a source of creativity. But if we can listen to our deeper soul desires for creative expression, I think we will begin to find new ways to offer our gifts and be paid as well. The challenge is to let our pride and expectations soften, so that our curiosity and creativity can find a fitting outer expression.

Assessing needs, however, goes beyond assessing financial requirements. We need to look carefully at the points where our energy seems fully engaged, where and with whom we feel supported and encouraged, and where the environment seems to suck energy out of us. We also need to ask ourselves, "How much time do I want to work? Am I willing to work on weekends? Travel? What benefits do I want in order to maintain my well-being?" These are questions any good career planning book will suggest, but they need to be asked in the larger context of discovering our gifts. Failure to ask these energetic questions will often result in feeling used, rather than useful.

We may want to work full-time for a short period, as my dad did, and then take a longer respite before taking on a new assignment. Other people will choose part-time work throughout the year. If we've been released from a demanding work schedule, we may have time and energy to learn something new or take on a new project. It sounds odd to our experienced ears, but being a beginner again can be creative—and fun.

Evaluating what we want to do and how many productive years we might expect will impact how ready we are to seek more training. If we already know that we like to work or enjoy a schedule that will take us out of the house, we can be more conscious about our choices.

What life experience and education we have is another factor. Because there are so many more healthy people with education and professional experience reaching retirement age now, there is a huge opportunity to make a difference in the communities where we have lived and worked. Old networks can become new opportunities to write or speak with the authority of our experience. One man who spent his prime years working on social justice issues on Capitol Hill is now writing a monthly blog on current policy issues for people who respect his judgment and don't have time to do the reading that he does.

Finally, we need to consider the needs of others in our family as we calculate the practical side of beginning new work. The career of our spouse or partner needs to be part of the picture, as well as any family members who depend on us for income or care. Looking at the whole package of who we are now can be a source of energy and courage. It can also help us avoid making choices to do nothing that we will later regret. Although a close look at our real needs can be difficult to do, it will save us from making avoidable mistakes and help us get to a full yes about what we want to do with our time and energy.

Assessing Abilities

Obviously, not everyone enjoys good health as they age. That does not mean we have reached the end of being able to contribute and grow, but we do need to think about what's ahead for us. We need to be realistic about what we can do and what we have to offer.

I think of Eileen. Suffering nerve damage from childhood trauma, she was living with constant bouts of vertigo and pain, which prevented her from holding a full-time job. She spent her early career as part of a medical team, designing proper nutrition for dialysis patients. Later, she got a PhD in anthropology and had planned to teach but her physical symptoms became debilitating. When her husband was unable to cope with her disabilities and left her, she decided to move into a retirement community, even though she was still in her sixties and was younger than most people there. She wanted a particular apartment because it would give her the light and exposure needed for growing orchids—something she undertook as she became more housebound. It took several years for that apartment to become available, but she used her time to get a financial settlement from her husband and to deepen her practice of Buddhist meditation and conscious pain management.

After assessing her prospects for some kind of useful work in the new retirement community, Eileen applied for training as a hospice volunteer. She was able to arrange for training in shorter blocks of time to accommodate her physical limitations. She now uses her medical background and many years of meditation to offer her quiet spirit at the bedside of one dying patient at a time. "I've even found a use for my orchids," she mused quietly, "because people quit sending flowers after a while." Eileen has found that even a person with dementia can respond to the beauty of an orchid, and it pleases her to share her lovely blooms that way. Her decision to assess her abilities and find ways to put them to use helped her cross the barrier of physical disability into creative aging.

Sometimes a realistic assessment of our abilities calls for some hard choices, but it may also make the path ahead clearer. Margaret had been a successful trial lawyer, following her father's footsteps toward becoming a judge, when she developed cancerous nodules on her vocal chords. She entered Jungian analysis to discover the meaning behind her health crisis and began creating large, colorful abstract paintings—an old love she had left behind in her climb up the state legal hierarchy. Determined to find a better balance for herself, she left her law practice and began doing mediation work through a restorative justice program at the local university. Evaluating her energy level and her need for some income, Margaret bought a smaller house and trimmed her work schedule. When I asked how she was able to maintain this new balance of using her education and experience for another purpose, she told of a dream group and a painting group where she gets ongoing encouragement for saying no to things that do not feed her soul.

Staying connected to the deeper streams of possibility that the inward journey provides can be a source of courage to face each day and make the necessary decisions, but it is hard to do that alone. Finding a place where we can be honest about our real needs is helpful. Although neither of Margaret's groups are directly connected to her restorative justice work, they feed her soul in other ways, helping her determine what she has the time and energy to do.

Clearing Space

Taking action to simplify our lives can be a positive activity at the threshold of retirement. Although some people avoid the thought of leaving the place where their children have grown up or the home where they have lived a significant portion of their adult lives, others find the challenge of downsizing part of their inner process for creative aging. Creating a new living space is not a long-term answer to the question of purpose in aging, but planning something new can be an invigorating project for the transition period. Making spatial decisions requires imagining future needs, assessing values, and discussing wishes and concerns of everyone involved.

When Larry and Jan noticed that the large house in which they raised three children had no bedroom on the first floor and that the steep stairs were getting harder to climb, they first joked about having a built-in StairMaster, but then realized they needed to make a change before it was forced on them. As they discussed their needs and wishes, they decided that they wanted more flexibility for their generative period than a planned retirement community would offer, so they decided to build a new house in a new development on the local golf course. As Larry and Jan designed a one-floor living space, they also made accommodations for a possible wheelchair, although they could hardly imagine themselves in that state. They chose a location near a university because they knew that cultural activity and physical exercise would be available there. They also added a downstairs apartment for visiting grandchildren now and for live-in help, if they needed assistance at a later time.

This couple used the new house to create a common work as they each transitioned from a busy career. It was a different kind of sabbatical project that helped them think creatively about their own aging. As they worked with the builder on their house, the rest of the development continued to expand. Other friends in their late fifties bought lots and began to build there as well. A couple who had been neighbors on the other side of town when all their children were preschoolers is now their next door neighbor, and they already know most of the people who are building on their street. Their move provided the opportunity to sort and simplify their things, and they are now both working again but with less demanding responsibilities.

Clearing space makes room for something new to develop. Sometimes we have the freedom to choose how and when that simplification process will take place. Sometimes it happens suddenly, with a move, job loss, or even bankruptcy. However it comes, pruning can be both painful and freeing. It all depends on whether we hang on to the loss or look ahead to what might be asking for room in the space that is now open and waiting.

Looking to Guides

Living into an uncertain future takes courage and hopefulness. Given the stream of negativity and fear that pours through the media, I think it's amazing that anyone has the courage to claim the "deep gladness" that we were born with. Most of us need help to do it.

A spiritual community where the message of death and new life are celebrated regularly is a valuable place to find support. Not only does the ritual of Holy Communion or Eucharist celebrate the crossing point between inner and outer experience, but also churches large and small tend to draw people who are attuned to seeking guidance through silence and prayerful listening. Spiritual Directors International is another source for finding trained listeners. Because our culture is so extroverted and productive, we don't have a tradition of seeking spiritual companionship for developmental transitions, but there is a growing body of knowledge for doing that. In Buddhist countries, young men typically spend time in a monastery before embarking on a career, and older men return to that life for a time of adjustment at the beginning of retirement. In our country, more people than ever are seeking new forms of contemplative practice that will assist them in making good choices for the creative period after full-time work.

Sometimes seasonal spiritual guides can be as close as our extended family. When my father closed his practice and began working on different Indian reservations, I could tell from his regular letters that he was learning new things about himself and feeling useful. For the next ten years, he took short-term assignments, setting bones and delivering babies for people who often traveled a hundred miles to the clinic where he was filling in for somebody more permanent. He often said that this generative decade was the most challenging and creative period of his medical practice. It was a model of generativity for me.

Other spiritual guides may surface in ways we don't expect. When Peter and I moved to northern Virginia, we had been eager to join the innovative Church of the Saviour. But when we arrived, we discovered that the founder, Gordon Cosby, had been preaching a message of change for the church. Instead of adopting the organizational pattern of "bigger is better," Gordon was urging a generation of new leadership to step forward and form smaller congregations, each with a particular mission. Then, instead of retiring from the scene, Gordon has continued to initiate one new mission after another, creating new models for low-income housing, advocating for health care for the homeless and those dying of AIDS, and providing job training for released prisoners and the chronically unemployed.

Another spiritual guide for me was M. C. Richards, the potter and painter who wrote (at midlife) the underground classic *Centering in Pottery, Poetry, and the Person*. Her writing helped me value handwork as a basic tool for understanding what it means to be fully human. In her sixties, she joined a Waldorf community in rural Pennsylvania, where she lived and worked with learning-disabled young adults. For her, farming gave rise to poetry, and cooking was as creative as a clay class. In her late sixties, she also joined the faculty of Matthew Fox's University of Creation Spirituality in Oakland, California. She taught there during the winter and went home to Camphill Village in Kimberton Hills, Pennsylvania, every spring in time to plant a garden. At seventy, she began making large, colorful paintings of images from her inner life. M. C. worked well into her eighties, inviting others into her final journey of conscious dying as her heart valves wore out. "It's a natural process," she once said to me, "which I don't choose to interrupt." She left as she had lived, embracing the reality of her soul.

Spiritual guides come in many guises. We see them everywhere when we look: a parent or rebel aunt, a pastor or professor, an older friend or a younger one who can stretch our thinking. These spiritual guides have made the crossing between desire and need, between their own deep gladness and the world's hunger for meaning and sustenance, and they can show others how to do it, too. If we let their lives beckon us to that crossing point, we will be able to find our call as well.

As I talked with different people about the actual transition from one modality of work to another, what surfaced was the importance of "wiggle room." In each case, people described a significant time period between one form of work and another, and some intentional practice of self-reflection. At the crossing point, when a new endeavor is becoming visible, it is also important to have some positive support.

Estimating our real needs can get us bogged down in planning rather than listening for inner guidance about when and how to move ahead. It's important to be realistic about assessing our abilities, as Eileen and Margaret were. It's also important to let our needs be a framework for our creativity, as Larry and Jan were able to do with their transition-year house project. Spiritual guides can show us how to cross from reflecting on who we are to acting and addressing a real need in the world, and can give us the courage to move ahead ourselves.

Spiritual Practice: Discernment

Crossing from the inner realm of possibility to the outer realm of action takes courage and trust. Going public with a deep desire to discover that place of wholeness means finding a trusted circle where you can name your experience of wholeness and be accepted without criticism, judgment, or advice. This circle could be friends, but it could also be people who are further down the road toward wholeness than you are.

Finding language for what may have been a sacred and wordless inner experience of belonging to a larger realm of spiritual connection can bring up deep fears from childhood—fears of breaking old taboos or unspoken rules, or even preverbal trauma from simply being who you were at an early age. But at this stage of life, hopefully you have enough confidence in yourself and the goodness of others to ask for what you need, even if you do not come from a religious tradition where this kind of practice is common.

A Quaker clearness committee, mentioned earlier, is a good model for supportive listening. Start by choosing three or four people who trust the inner guidance of spirit and who are conscious enough to keep from giving advice. Choose a facilitator who can hold the silence and remind people of the group's intention to listen for guidance together. To do that, it's helpful to meet in dim light and keep eyes closed or downcast to avoid moving into a traditional question-and-answer mode.

Begin with at least ten minutes of silence. Then articulate your question briefly. The role of the group is to ask questions that are truly open, such as "What makes you smile?" rather than "Have you considered...?" Let yourself respond spontaneously, without censorship. Allow a significant breathing space before the next question, so the group keeps the whole process right at the edge of silence. It's helpful to have someone taking notes, so neither you nor the group is trying to remember what is said.

When the facilitator senses that the process has reached a natural conclusion, he or she might ask the group to hold the process in silence for a few more minutes. Then if you have anything else to say, that would bring the process of deep listening to a close.

This process is not meant to solve problems or reach a neat conclusion. It is an open-ended practice of listening for inner guidance, trusting in the presence of divine love.

Questions to Ponder

1. How would you describe the tension between your hopeful vision for the future and your current reality?

2. How would you describe your deep gladness now?

3. What is a deep hunger in the world that touches you?

4. Create a list of people who have been guides and mentors. Write a brief description of the top five. Imagine that you are meeting with each one and ask them for guidance at this time in your life. Write down what you hear, even if it makes no sense right now.

7

RISK
Beginning Again with More Focus

> Each of us has, in our imaginations and memories,
> images of freedom against the odds.
> —David Whyte, *Crossing the Unknown Sea*

Springtime for the soul is full of risk. Buds burst into bloom too early. A chilly wind nips new shoots of green with frost. By afternoon, warm sun welcomes what we have been afraid to offer. We have completed the inner work of endings and the neutral zone. Finally, we are ready to be our true selves in public.

Risk is the opening phase of new beginnings. It is a time for shaping and forming our work from the fire in our hearts. No longer so firmly tied to the expectations of others, we are ready to set forth with an inner compass. Trusting our own instincts about what matters most, we step out into the world after a sabbatical period, so our compassion, knowing, and sometimes extraordinary sacrifice for a larger good can flow. A grandmother takes on care of a grandchild who would otherwise be homeless. An elder gathers his energy to speak at a public gathering, like Ted Kennedy who spoke at his party's nominating convention even though he knew the cost to his health could be dear.

In less dramatic ways, people everywhere confront old stereotypes and step beyond barriers because they believe in their power to make a difference. A truck driver trades his big rig for a pickup and develops a small business delivering groceries. A computer specialist shifts her energy to offer her expertise in an afterschool program. A government bureaucrat studies acupuncture because she wants to have more personal contact with people and to help her clients stay healthy.

Beginning a new form of work takes courage and trust in ourselves. It also requires trust that our lives unfold out of small openings. Our desire to be useful can lead to volunteer positions, which then morph into paying jobs. Personal qualities can augment our skills as we discover how we are needed by others. And sometimes our needs and disabilities give us a different viewpoint, a slant on life that becomes generative. The risk of going public with who we are and what we most want to see change in the world around us can be both exciting and intimidating at the same time. As we come to the point of beginning an encore career, whatever we have held close and were afraid to expose to others now breaks into public view.

The risk of beginning an encore career brings with it all the hopes and fears of the first day of school. We don't know how it will turn out, but we must begin with one step forward, then another, then another. We cannot wait around for somebody else to initiate what we vaguely dream about; that may never happen. Instead, we must start where we are, with what we have, and move toward the dream we hold of the world we want to live in. In fact, the only way that something new is born into the world is when a particular human being thinks of it and then has the courage to act.

Resilience

Our ability to risk a new venture at this stage of life depends a lot on whether we have cultivated fear or trust in earlier years. It depends on how much we have grown in our capacity for resilience over time through events that have tested our tolerance and flexibility again and again. Some people become brittle and afraid; others become more supple and trusting. Some have coped with economic necessity and know themselves to be resourceful and positive. Others have felt pinched and burdened by the same circumstances.

Some of that is inborn temperament, and some derives from early experiences of trust, love, and safety—or mistrust bred of too much early comparison and criticism.

Our spirit of adventure and tolerance for risk is usually cultivated at home, during childhood. When our parents told stories of their early years, they passed on values even before we had language for such things. If our parents were timid and fearful, that's the story we heard and have to overcome. But even if our parents did not show us how to initiate new work in our later years, this does not mean we are crippled for life. In fact, there are books and people all around us who are modeling generativity, and we can learn from them. If, on the other hand, our parents were brave and resourceful, we may find it easier to start something new. More often, we have inherited some of each quality, and the inner work we have done previously will determine how ready we are to risk starting something new at this stage.

My dad provided a model of courageous initiative for me. I grew up hearing about his decision to take money that his mother had managed to save as a seamstress and leave for college, even though his father wanted him to stay home and work in construction. He worked his way through several failures, never received any more financial support from his parents, and finished his formal education with a medical degree from Stanford, although it took him until he was thirty. I learned from his stories and actions that perseverance, humility, and common sense are trustworthy guides. His resilience and resourcefulness have been an encouragement for me.

Our feelings about risk are also shaped by our own life experiences. If we have been sheltered by marriage or wealth, the thought of starting out alone on a new venture may feel too risky and overwhelming. Fear can also take hold as we age and our sense of physical potency declines. Advertisements play on those fears, and we are bombarded with warnings about the pitfalls of not saving enough for retirement. Fear promotes stagnation because we tend to live reactively, too worried to risk much of anything. The task at hand is twofold: how to protect ourselves from the torrent of negativity that inflates fear and how to cultivate experiences of trust and originality.

Although the way we approach risk may have begun in childhood, life and circumstances also teach us how, or how not, to become the creative force we were born to be. The quality of resilience can be an acquired skill.

Carolyn is optimistic and proactive, but her path has not been an easy one. A graduate of Union Theological Seminary in New York City, she was a volunteer Christian educator in the United Church of Christ while she and her husband, a college professor, raised their two girls. Then, when her husband left the marriage, she went to work selling commercial printing because it was something she could do. Although it was not the career she'd prepared for, she was extroverted and well organized enough to earn a solid living for herself once her girls were launched.

As the printing business changed with new technologies, Carolyn moved to a bigger company where she had to cover a larger sales territory. There, the pressures of her work increased with more customers and less control over the products she was selling. She had to stretch, adjust, and adapt. She had less time to develop the working relationships that she valued, and she wondered if she should look for other work. Though her desire might have been to leave her job at that point, the reality was that she needed the health insurance until Medicare coverage made retirement a viable option.

When Carolyn was able to retire, she expressed her desire to "wake without an alarm clock, drink coffee as long as I like, and read a book in the morning." But she also knew that she needed to be around people, so she applied for a part-time job at a Cokesbury bookstore. The job is a good fit for her: she enjoys being a resource for people, her organizational skills are used in managing inventory, and the job gives her just enough extra income to travel. Yet, there was still a missing piece—one that would take more of a risk.

Carolyn was also searching for a role in the church where she could use her education and experience. When a new pastor arrived, the church began to attract new members, and its "open and affirming" stance brought in several talented gay and transgendered younger people. Carolyn wondered if she would feel marginalized as a single, straight, older woman. Her resilience was tested as she debated whether to leave or stay. She decided to step into her own questions by serving a term as a moderator of the church and found that others, including the new pastor, valued her theological training and administrative skills. Then, when her term ended, she felt restless and uncertain again.

A letter from the denomination proved to be a turning point. Ten years earlier, Carolyn had secured a credential allowing her to preach and perform sacraments. Nothing had ever come of that application, and now the denomination was asking her to cancel or renew. As the deadline approached, she began to dream about creating a new position for herself at the church. She sought help from friends and her spiritual director, wondering if she dared to ask for official recognition. Finally, she decided to risk asking for what she wanted from the church and the denomination. She wrote her own job description to become the Minister for Equipping Saints and proposed an eight-hour-a-week position, with reviews at six months and a year, to determine whether she and the congregation felt it was a good fit. Although it was to be unpaid, she wanted official confirmation because it gave her more credibility with the congregation.

Carolyn trusted her hard-earned resilience as she entered this new territory. From her earliest working days, when she started at the printing company out of necessity, to her adaptations as technology changed, she had already practiced and honed her ability to be flexible about her work. She knew and understood what some of her gifts were and was ready to risk offering them in a new setting, but she wisely chose not to try it alone. "The most important thing in developing this new position," she said, "is my support group. We gather with silent prayer, then I give a ten-minute report and name issues that I want their help with. We sit in silence, listening for guidance together and finally share what our leadings have been. I don't feel alone. I think we're developing this ministry together."

The association has reactivated her commission status, and Carolyn is now being paid for part-time church work that was once only a dream. Because she was willing to make practical choices and live modestly and trust her inner guidance about timing and risk, she has found herself with an encore career that spans bookstore and church. "I wanted some time to be a grandmother," she added, "but not too much. I think I've got just the right balance for now."

Desire to Be Useful

As I interviewed people for this book, we talked about the difference between stagnation and generativity. A single phrase came up almost every time: "I want to be useful, but not feel used or taken for granted." There is a group in Pueblo, Colorado, called The Eccentrics, who have developed this question of usefulness into an identity. They meet every other week in the back room of a restaurant. There are no dues or bylaws, and every person pays for his or her own lunch. The Eccentrics invite a public official to attend, and they spend about twenty minutes asking that person intelligent, thoughtful questions. One official said, "They don't seem to have an agenda or party bias. Nobody else has asked me such good questions. When I speak with this group, I learn some of the questions I need to be asking myself."

Being useful and creative without feeling burdened by the expectations or ambitions of others involves both self-awareness and a sense of connection with some wider community or tradition. In his book *Good Work*, economist E. F. Schumacher describes good work as providing useful goods and services, developing our gifts, and working with others. The need to find some useful work at every stage of life seems basic to me. Paid or unpaid, work brings meaning to our lives, even though the content or definitions of work changes as we age. As our sense of the limits of time and life energy becomes more urgent, what is truly useful becomes more important.

Over our years of work, promotions may have lured us away from the passion that once drew us to a particular field or work. We may find ourselves going through the motions, meeting requirements that seem to have little connection to the real work that we see needs to be done in the world. When we reach the generative stage, we may begin to question where we are spending our energy and on what. We become more critical and thoughtful about our choices. If we are paying attention to the wider framework of values and our own internal wholeness, we are better able to see what is truly useful.

Our culture's current retirement patterns seem to encourage stagnation rather than usefulness. The message seems to be: "You've worked hard. Now it's time to retire to a gated community, with occasional jaunts for travel and visits with grandchildren." There is little or no attention to the need for meaningful work. If we settle for this, we may become a caricature, an aging cartoon, of the younger person we once were who arrived determined to make a difference in the world.

Fortunately, our souls rebel.

If we are willing to risk stepping into a new environment and deliberately put ourselves into cooperative working situations, we will have opportunities to nurture neglected parts of ourselves that we have been too busy to attend to at earlier stages. We will continue learning new things about ourselves and those around us.

I think of Bill, whom I met at a church retreat. He had never had time to attend a retreat before. He had worked as an accountant for many years, making sure that payroll and deduction amounts were accurate. He was proud of his accuracy and knowledge of financial systems but felt that he wanted more human contact in his work. He knew that he enjoyed teaching newcomers how to do their jobs well and thought he might want to become a high school teacher if and when he retired.

When his company offered an early retirement package, Bill took it and began to research local certification programs for high school math teachers, but there were no openings in areas that he felt competent to teach. About the same time, there was an announcement at his church that the local food bank was looking for a part-time accountant, so he applied for the job and got it. Now Bill is working two days a week at the food bank and is beginning to volunteer there, doing other things as well. Although he really wanted to work more hours and never imagined himself at a food bank, Bill decided to risk letting a way open for him rather than planning it all out.

Right now, Bill's volunteer work at the food bank is satisfying his desire for teamwork, and he has just signed up for a management course at the community college because he has noticed some other organizational needs involving collection and distribution of food. As we spoke, I could see the excitement and challenge he was feeling about his new work.

There is no question in Bill's mind that his work is needed and useful, and by shortening his work hours and volunteering with others from his church, he has put himself in a position to expand his social network in a healthy way. The risk for him was trusting his desire to help others as well as his need for more human contact.

Focus on Gifts

Trusting our gifts at this stage of life can be a hazard, a risky gamble in favor of soul over perceived safety. What we once thought of as the security of our skills will be challenged, softened, stretched, and shaped into a new form. Shedding the identity of a former position can mean stepping out without a shield. Coming home to the true self is both a source of new inspiration and a fearful kind of vulnerability.

To risk being less than others thought we were is one of the greatest risks we can take. Owning the reality of our health, energy, interests, and financial resources means separating from the idealized image of how life ought to be. It means letting go of our expectations and shedding the persona that promised "happily ever after."

Instead, the true self is ready to focus on who we are now, in this time and place. We tend to think of "gifts" as special talents or abilities, but it is also our gift of responsiveness, of aliveness, that has much to offer other people. Even a baby, with no skills at all, can be a gift. Notice the way people respond when a baby is brought into a waiting room, the way he or she draws people out of their usual cocoon of privacy. If we can extend this awareness to every person and see the gifts each brings to a particular endeavor, we will be on our way to understanding the key to generativity.

The notion that everyone has a gift for the good of the whole community is not something our individualistic culture teaches us, but rather is something from the biblical tradition of communal identity. When the Apostle Paul wrote to the churches at Ephesus, Corinth, and Rome, he taught that gifts were given to each person for a different purpose, but that all gifts were for the common good. According to Paul, the work of the church was to help people find and use their particular gifts.

This was the task that Marilyn faced. She had been a nurse before her children arrived, and now that her children were grown, she wanted to explore some of the health-care needs in her community. She felt that she had completed most of her work as a mother, and she was ready for a new challenge. But she feared her marriage would be at risk if she pursued her dream, and she was nervous about describing what she wanted to do. Her husband provided them with a comfortable living, and he could not understand why she wanted to complicate their lives by taking on a "thankless job" (his words). He wanted her to be home and waiting when he came back from his demanding law practice.

Sometimes we will need to leave the comfort of a close network of family and friends to strike out in a new direction. The risk is that old friends or a spouse will not understand or accept our newfound passion and will sabotage the effort of starting something new. Taking a stand or striking out in a new direction can put relationships at risk. For Marilyn, the path to using her gifts meant introducing change incrementally, to lessen the risk of rupture at home. She found support for her larger sense of call by taking on smaller challenges, such as taking leadership for the blood drive at the high school. Her husband was more understanding about her responsibilities there, and she was able to focus on developing her combination of nursing experience and desire to help people in the community.

When we have the opportunity for developing our underused gifts, paying attention to the level of doing what we love is important. Too small a focus feels like selfishness. Too large a focus ("I'll do *anything*") undercuts a desire for pride and excellence in honing our skills. If we are too passive about our particular gifts, we don't experience the pleasure of using our gifts well. The challenge of being specific, accountable, and responsible for something we care about passionately is both a risk and a reward.

Perfecting our gifts can be a lifelong pursuit, but as we soften toward sixty, we can let the driving and striving period loosen its grip a bit and discover what other forms our gifts might take. As a government lawyer, Dick always had an opinion about what others ought to be doing. As he aged, he began to recognize he could not be perfect no matter how hard he tried, and he began to be more tolerant of others. Finally, as he lived through the death of his father and the decline of his mother, I noticed that he was becoming more humble and accepting of his own failings and those of others, too. Now, as Dick is approaching retirement from his official position, he seems much more ready to do something that will be less visible and more useful to others. He is more ready to shuck the shell of his official position and offer help to others, doing carpentry for an aging neighbor and filling in as a volunteer scoutmaster.

Letting go of our professional identity and claiming a new, more human one is a huge step for most of us. The risk of naming who we are without reference to a job title or a professional degree means that we have truly done the inner work of release. Instead of wanting others to believe in us and acknowledge our capabilities, which often happens during the second (vocational) round of call, we arrive at a new identity as the person we have now become. What I know from my own experience is how hard it is to keep from being introduced as a "former" somebody—"she was the former director" or "she was the editor and publisher"—rather than who I am now. It's not that earlier accomplishments can't be mentioned, but in the third round of call, we need to stand on our own feet, be present to our own life and the gifts of our experience, and let that be enough. That's the risk of going public with what we want to be doing at this stage of life.

Liberation from Egocentricity

Schumacher's description of good work includes working with others "to liberate ourselves from our inborn egocentricity." It's natural for every child to think he or she is the center of the universe. Although there is a certain element of being liberated from our egocentricity by belonging to a family, a tribe, or a religious tradition, the first round of call we face as young adults is to wrestle with the question, "Who am I?" We need to do the inner work of claiming our identity, which actually requires strengthening the ego.

During the second round of call, when we are sorting out "What is my work?" we are also building ego strength, though it focuses on vocation and recognition by others. We want to be useful and creative, and when we are rewarded for that, our work becomes an expression of who we are.

But as we age and our souls get restless to develop other parts of our lives that have waited in the shadows, going public with a new venture can seem terribly risky, even threatening to the identity we have held previously. By this time in our lives, even if we have done the inner work of release and reclamation, going public with a new kind of work may feel shameful and diminished because it is likely to be more personal, more human, and more based on recognizing our interdependence rather than a hierarchy. Letting go of our former credibility and position is the real risk of claiming a new beginning at this stage of life.

Good work with others teaches us about the interdependence of all things. Working together in new, creative ways can invite us to take our rightful place in the family of human beings, each with a claim to our common resources. Something as simple and needed as volunteering at a local food bank can put us in a place where we must solve practical problems together for a common purpose. We must attend, adjust, pitch in, and go the extra mile again and again. We learn not only to tolerate each other, but sometimes to love each other as well. At the core, that's what it means to move beyond egocentricity.

Taking the risk to be who we are in public can be the seed for new life, new energy, and a new call. After the straightjacket of a stressful career, the generative years may begin with feelings of being naked and unknown. Without the old roles to determine who we are and what we say when somebody asks, "And what do you do?," the risk of moving beyond our professional masks to a life, as Parker J. Palmer says, "divided no more," is both exhilarating and terrifying. We will need to find others with similar goals, to plant our roots in good soil in order to offer our gifts to others.

Palmer tells the poignant story of his own risk in his book *A Hidden Wholeness*. In his early sixties, he realized that his professional life as a writer and lecturer needed to end, but he was afraid of being "a seventy-year-old man who does not know who he is when the books are out of print and the audiences are no longer applauding." Once he heard himself say those words, he knew they were true, and he began crafting a plan, not so much to find other work as to discover his true self. What he was able to discern with the help of others has resulted in new work that does not involve endless travel. He is now training others to lead "circles of trust" based on (but not limited to) the Quaker practice of clearness committees for mutual discernment.

❦

The risk of starting something new in your encore years can be both fearful and exhilarating. Success is no longer the primary question. When we find the good work that is ours to do at this stage of life, we will discover our resilience and adaptability in fresh ways, as Carolyn did. We can find real joy in being useful in the community of ordinary people that surrounds us wherever we are, as Bill did when he volunteered at a local food bank and saw that there were needs he could fill. In moving beyond the egocentricity of any professional career, we can discover new gifts of presence and personhood that will take us beyond our learned skills, as Dick was able to do.

Stepping into the risk of new work that our culture does not yet recognize as essential is an act requiring creativity and imagination. Liberation is a process of letting our public persona be replaced by the flawed, yet creative person that each of us is at the core. Discovering the unique gift of our *true self* is both the risk and the reward.

Spiritual Practice: A Rule for Life

As you take the risk of going public with your true self, you might find it helpful to develop a personal mission statement or "a rule for life," as Saint Benedict called it. Basically, it involves naming what is most important to you in life and using these points as your spiritual compass. Like the ancient monastic practice of the Rule of Saint Benedict, your "rule" should be both visionary and practical, brief and doable. One woman came up with these four elements as her "rule" for her generative years:

1. Live close to God by setting aside time to walk and be with God each morning.
2. Be creative and have fun rather than turning into a scold.
3. Stay healthy and have some adventures.
4. Share myself with others wherever I am.

After this woman had named her guidelines aloud, she added brightly: "The good news is that I can take these goals into old age with me as well."

As you consider what is most important to you, you might think first of daily issues, and then expand to a larger time frame and a larger context than your home and family. Don't try to include too much, however; start with a few core essentials. You may want to expand your "rule" over time, but it's better to give yourself a chance to integrate each addition fully into how you live and work and play before adding another.

Questions to Ponder

1. What part of your life is asking to be born right now? Is there some risk in that for you?
2. How would you describe your "resilience quotient"? What has helped you strengthen your resilience? To be more flexible? To develop a certain hardiness?

3. What kind of work did you consider "useful" in the previous decade? How has that changed? What do you consider "useful" now?

4. What would it take for you to let others help you with discernment?

8

RELATING
Finding the Right Form for Now

New feet within my garden go—
New fingers stir the sod.
A troubadour upon the elm
Betrays the solitude.
—Emily Dickinson

Relating, the final phase of the third round of call, is the time to water and fertilize whatever sprout of new work we identified in the early spring season of risk. It's time to tend the surrounding garden—till the soil, clear the weeds, and prune the spindly runners so our work can mature and reach its full potential. It is the season for finding or creating a web of relationships or an organizational structure for sharing our sense of call with others.

Whatever gift we bear into the world with our aging bodies, it is meant to be shared. Connecting with others is the way in which we offer the work of our hands and the hope of our hearts. Relating marks the nexus between what we want to give and what others need to have. Our desire to be connected could be as simple as designing a website or as complicated as starting a new business.

As we step fully into the new beginning of this encore phase of life, we will be more conscious of physical limits, more careful about the way we spend energy, resources, and time. And we are more likely to give ourselves freely where it matters most. Identifying where and how we want to offer ourselves wholeheartedly is the mission of encore work. Figuring out how to embody the ripened experience of conscious aging is the challenge.

Relating encompasses all the different ways we feel useful and engaged with others. It is the outer expression of what we have learned from the inner work of reclamation and revelation and the natural extension of what we have chosen to claim publicly, something we are ready to give. This phase is a rich time for relationships, for belonging and community. It is a time to claim the authority of aging, to do the work we were made for, and to enjoy the fullness of our unique gifts. If we have done the inner work of the preceding seasons, relating is a natural extension of some new creative impulse or seed of an idea as it takes root in community.

Creating Community

In this generative period, we have a chance to deepen social connections and make a contribution to others—a primary factor in aging well, according to psychiatrist George Vaillant in his famous longitudinal Harvard study of adult development. If we can bring that desire for social connection and community into our work by offering our skills and experience in new ways, we will begin to affect the fabric of our culture. This is one of the marks of creative aging: offering ourselves for some larger purpose rather than protecting what we've got. We want to make a difference, leave a legacy, enjoy the substance of our uniqueness as we age.

Finding or building a community takes effort and vision to act on shared values. Technology gives us a sense of connection throughout the world, and yet we still long for places to belong, to call "home." Entrepreneurs can find an audience through the Web, and neighborhood websites can pass along information about everything from local contractors to petty crime, but the willingness to participate often depends on an "on-site" person—a neighbor who will host a yard party to bring in newcomers, a volunteer who will meet with helpers to iron out the necessary details of a project, a woman who will provide food that will nourish other volunteer workers. Although the Internet gives us more ways to share information, it is no substitute for face-to-face encounters, which nurture a sense of community and love and encourage giving. Many are wrestling with the pros and cons of the Web. Is virtual community enough? How can we cultivate respect without knowing our neighbors or sharing common values? How do we encourage shared values and care for the common good?

Although women have often carried the habits of local community into the workplace—remembering birthdays and asking after pictures on the cubicle wall—we are still in the process of figuring out how to nurture community in a mobile society beyond creating more rules and regulations. Constant economic and social change can be stimulating if there is a core of stability somewhere. But as the current generation of elders who nurtured relationships in local neighborhoods move to retirement complexes, we will depend more and more on those who understand the need for personal contact.

Paul and Sharon had bought a large house when they married. After their children grew up and moved on, they decided to offer their house for anyone who needed a place to live. Their rule was simple: we have a room and a bed to offer; the rest is up to you. As a busy lawyer, Sharon did not want to be cooking for a crowd or cleaning up after capable adults, but she and Paul were willing to offer housing as a basic necessity for creating community.

A young hospice chaplain who wanted to live simply and spend his time writing music moved in. That arrangement went well for several years. Then the real challenge came. John, a homeless man who was trying to stay sober, needed a place to stay. Paul and Sharon were wary but willing. In a short-term contract with John, they offered him a room but soon realized that his needs might overwhelm them. In this microcommunity, everyone had a steep learning curve as they struggled to find common ground and a common set of rules to live by. Paul and Sharon asked for help from their church community. People stepped in with specific skills. One man agreed to sponsor John in Alcoholics Anonymous (AA), another helped John make business cards, and others offered

John companionship so Paul and Sharon would not be his sole community.

John is now renting a room in another house. He has his ten-month chip from AA to honor his sobriety, and he has just bought a used van to expand his pet-care business. Paul and Sharon have established a good friendship with John now that he is more independent, and everyone involved has learned by experience how to create more conscious boundaries in the effort to build a functional community. Relating takes practice and intention, something every parent learns, but when we extend our caring to others who are not directly related by blood or marriage, need can become the nexus for healing and community.

Personal Connections

I think it was Maggie Kuhn, founder of the Gray Panthers, who made Florence Kennedy's slogan "Don't agonize, organize!" so famous. But people in the generative stage of life have often spent twenty or thirty years in an organization, and they are tired of meeting somebody else's goals and expectations. All too often, as the organizations they worked for have grown, the structures have become more complex, and their work has involved more paper and less personal contact.

Most of the people I interviewed for this book confessed that they were not really looking for another job in a hierarchy, particularly if they had been working in a large bureaucracy. Instead, they were looking for a small, flexible organization where they would have more hands-on work and time for reconnecting with people or for exploring some of the creative reserves that had been lurking around the edges with no time for development.

When I spoke with Janet, she had already taken the risk of leaving a managerial position because she didn't like the person she had become in that job. She wanted to reclaim the passion that had originally brought her into doing physical therapy and make more space in her life for contributing other things in her community.

Janet grew up on an island off the coast of Maine, where her mother was a nurse. She remembers as a girl seeing an ad on television for a physical therapist on the hospital ship *Hope*. The description captured her imagination even at a young age. Her mother arranged for her to meet a physical therapist at the county hospital where she could see what was involved, and her desire to become a therapist grew. She got the education she needed and started work in a hospital, but found that she loved seeing patients at home so she could encourage overall wellness.

Risking her salary to join a nascent home-health-care agency, Janet reduced her workload to twenty hours a week. Within two years, the agency expanded to three therapists, and she was able to work full-time, combining patient care with supervision of the other therapists. By the time I talked with her, she was managing the scheduling and training for twenty-three home-health therapists. Although she liked her work well enough, she felt pressured by paperwork. As federal regulations increased and money tightened, the working environment changed. She stewed for months, unhappy and unsure what to do. "I didn't like me anymore," she said. "I was crotchety at work and at home, too."

Janet had always been a caretaker, but increasing regulations required a different management style. She was asked to be less personally involved and more businesslike, but that pushed against her sense of herself. She enjoyed the variety of her work (training, scheduling, keeping up with health-care needs in a growing community) and the good working relationships that she had with "her" therapists, but she also recognized that her style of management was "old-fashioned" and too "motherly" for the current business climate. When key people on her management team were replaced and the flexibility she had enjoyed was taken away, her satisfaction drained away. She was ready to leave.

When Janet gave notice, the new administrator was floored. Janet reported, "She let me know that they would do almost anything to keep me on in some capacity, so after a three-month break, I'm going back to work on a per diem basis doing direct patient care again." Janet is also looking forward to having some volunteer time to give at the local humane society and as a trustee for her church. And, with a twinkle in her eye, she told me, "I'm even thinking of having a table at the weekly craft fair," but she wouldn't tell me what she might be selling. "It needs to be a surprise so somebody else doesn't do it," she smiled. Her creative spirit was eager for expression in all those different ways.

Like Janet, many women are finding that the economic and political skills they have learned—often needed to push patriarchal systems for equal pay for equal work—can now be turned into more flexible people skills in their organizations. Rather than competing with younger workers who bring new knowledge and skills into the workplace, older workers can provide wisdom and guidance—if they are not pressured out of the workplace.

Women who have been used to juggling family and work needs throughout their careers will find new opportunities to provide hands-on service—*if* we don't drown them with regulation and litigation before they get started. As a society, we will have to restrain our fears and let love find a way to offer itself in new forms. Sometimes that simply means functioning in smaller units so we can know and trust each other.

George Vaillant, in his book *Aging Well,* tells the story of a carpenter with the Massachusetts Department of Public Works who had worked his way up to be the shop steward of the union. He explained to the Harvard study interviewer that his bosses realized that they needed his experience with people as well as his job skills, and so they were treating him better. He spoke to the interviewer with authority and ease even though predictions based on early IQ tests would not have anticipated his success. Like Janet, he brought good parental experience to the workplace and discovered how much these personal qualities were needed and valued.

As the workplace becomes more data driven, the question of where and how to meet our needs for human contact will become even more important. Organizations are going to need people with good connecting skills.

Direct Service

One of the recurrent themes among people whom I interviewed for this book was how often their dedication and skill on the job were recognized with promotions from direct service into management. Many of us have experienced this movement from direct personal involvement to teaching or supervising others who are actually doing the work. Over time, we move away from direct results of our work, whether that is healing or teaching or manipulating materials, which once gave us concrete feedback and the satisfaction of doing something skillfully.

I once taught history and English in junior high school, then moved to high school, and then to counseling at the college level. It felt like movement from hand to head. As a corrective, perhaps, I began working with clay in my spare time, gradually becoming a professional potter. It wasn't long, though, before people wanted me to teach them how to throw, glaze, and fire their pots, and I had less and less time for my own production. The same phenomenon happened when I was hired to be the director of Faith At Work. Once again, I moved away from doing the work myself to teaching others how to do it.

Now, as I enter this third round of call, I am more like the man who buried his one talent in the ground. As I dig it up from the clay bank where I buried the artistic dreamer that I once was, I realize that the master I serve is not harsh and demanding after all. Money and recognition are no longer the needs they once were for me. I can put my hands back into the clay, making a clay burial urn for someone I love, and not worry much about neglecting other commitments. I can also choose to spend my time offering the simple gift of my presence to someone who needs it. They don't care about my credentials or previous success, and more important, I don't need to let them know.

In our culture, direct service commands the least respect— except from those receiving it. I am grateful for the mechanic who keeps my car running, the plumber who figured out where the leak in the pipe was, the roofer who repaired storm damage when a tree blew down onto the roof, the carpenter who built our deck. It's ironic: none of those skills can be outsourced, and yet we do not encourage young people to get those basic skills. I think of Jim, who discovered on the Guatemalan pilgrimage not only his love for helping people directly but also how satisfying it can be to solve a service problem that actually has a solution rather than spending time worrying about sales volume and management training. The headaches of management were what he needed to retire from, not the social structure of his work.

People who have commanded respect as teachers and managers can change our attitudes toward direct service if they get involved in offering direct service themselves. Men who will teach shop and woodworking skills to latchkey kids after school might go a long way toward easing some of the tensions that encourage gangs. Women who have run successful businesses might turn their attention to better care for the very old and the very young—and while they are at it, find creative ways to cultivate beauty, drama, and music as well.

Direct service will never bring the financial and social rewards that we offer sports stars or financial gurus. But as an encore career, hands-on helping makes a community more whole and healthy, more connected and vital. A connection between our deep gladness and the real needs in a community calls forth this generative expression of our creative energies.

Public Service

We sometimes make fun of old-fashioned women who "need to feed" whenever someone comes to visit, but the opposite is much more distressing. When women are so narrowed by corporate careers that they literally do not know how to feed others, physically or relationally, everyone suffers. I am hopeful that women in this third round of call will find new ways to bring those caring services to their local communities as they step back from bureaucratic responsibilities and still have eyes to see the needs around them.

I had to schedule time to talk with a sixty-two-year-old city council member several different times in order to accommodate her busy schedule of community meetings. Jill had spent the first twenty years of her married life raising three energetic children. Then she was ready for another career. At that time, her husband ran a car dealership, which he had purchased from his father. Japanese cars were just entering the American market in large numbers, so Jill took a management course and started a Honda dealership across the street from her husband's store. She was determined to make her dealership friendly for professional women, and her strategy soon paid off with a strong reputation for sales and service.

By the millennium, Jill was elected the first female president of the American International Automotive Dealers Association (AIADA). She was fifty-three years old then and feeling her oats in a business dominated by men. Although the AIADA was much smaller than the parallel domestic car association, she became an industry spokesperson and a model for younger women in that business. Then, the question of succession raised the possibility of early retirement to give their son control of the family business, and she looked around for some local place to channel her energy and experience.

For this retired businesswoman, public office offered a chance to model the changes she wanted to see in her city. Jill decided to run for an open seat on the city council. She declared from the beginning that she would only serve one four-year term. She and another woman who ran at the same time were determined to bring better accountability to the "old boy network." They stirred up a hornets' nest as they challenged the network of assumed privileges and used their "mothering skills" to invite more cooperation. They pushed for greater accountability by city employees and council members, targeted services in underserved neighborhoods, advocated for beautification as well as careful spending, and actively sought cooperation of a nearby military installation on water quality. As a one-term council member, Jill brought the enthusiasm of a newcomer and the practical skills of a community organizer to what became a full-time job for little pay. "I wish everyone would find a place to give their expertise somewhere in the community," she concluded, as we finished our interview.

As she got involved in the political terrain, Jill had noticed the barren parks in the physical landscape. An avid gardener, she invited some of her gardening friends to tackle neglected medians and triangle parks owned by the city. She got orange T-shirts for these Wednesday Weeders and promised to limit their efforts to three hours every week. This loyal cadre of weeders convinced the parks and recreation department to plant water-wise plantings that would require less maintenance in the future. What began as an effort to absent herself from the day-to-day management of the motor company became a deep commitment to the welfare of her community.

Public service can take many forms, and we do not need to be limited to the jobs that already exist. It's often up to us to create a needed structure. If we have done the inner work to reclaim and reorient our passions, we will be more ready to create a new form that fits the situation where we find ourselves, and our work will continue to unfold as we age. What we did for fun and profit at forty will not be the same as what satisfies us at sixty or seventy. Finding the things we are willing to offer in a more transitory venue can provide a creative field of human relationships in which we can follow the leads that open up. Working from the heart often takes us where we didn't plan to go, but if we are to live wholeheartedly, giving our time, energy, and money to the work that is ours to do, we will have to commit ourselves to the places where we are called to give our best with no guarantee of permanence or success.

Responding to Need

At this time in history, many of us have been given the gift of extra years in good health, and we have a greater awareness of the needs all around us. They cry out for creative answers. If we have been "too busy" at the peak of our careers to find time for volunteer efforts, we now have a new opportunity to respond to the needs at hand, whether they be a hungry neighbor, a hurting teen, or our ailing planet.

As an Episcopal priest, Pat had been a social activist in his prime, promoting fair housing and intentional community in New York City. He retired early because of serious health problems, but agreed to fill a temporary, part-time position as rector for a poor urban church. After five years, he is still there.

The tiny stone chapel is on a corner between two huge cathedrals, once crowded with French and Italian mill hands working in the textile factories. Both stand empty now. On a recent visit, people in various states of need crowded around the basement door, smoking, talking quietly, or just waiting. Upstairs, the sanctuary was empty—except for the majestic sounds of a Russian male choir. As the basso voices rolled through the carved archways, I noticed a solitary figure in his black robe, completely absorbed. I watched for a long time, taking in the beauty of the dark wood, the Tiffany windows, and an ornate oriental rug next to the altar. When Pat noticed me, he switched off the sound system and said quietly, "Sorry. That's how I prepare myself for worship." We made our introductions, and I sat down in front, awaiting my turn to preach.

As worship began, I noticed that we were using worship folders instead of prayer books to make the service easier to follow. The musicians improvised each week, depending on who showed up. This week there was a jazz pianist, a drummer, a clarinetist, and a violinist. The congregation was sparse and scattered in the chilled nave. When it was time for the Eucharist, Pat called people by name to come forward and join in a circle, gathering us like a flock on that beautiful rug by the altar. Again he called us by name as he offered the Eucharist, somehow channeling love and redemption from a greater source in this unlikely place. The flock was young and old; black, brown, and white; well dressed and destitute. And here was a portly priest with a bum heart, who lived alone in a trailer, able to offer himself where he was most needed.

Relating means making connections, putting the unique gifts of one person in touch with the needs of another. And the relating at this little church didn't begin and end with Pat. The person in the central office who had called Pat out of retirement was an evocator, one who summons or calls forth. This person recognized something in Pat and made an essential link, weaving the fabric of spiritual community out of the gossamer thread of inspiration. Whoever that was, was an artist of relating.

Sharing Resources

Another aspect of creating community is recognizing the needs of those at the margins. Sharing resources comes more naturally when we know one another. The tiny congregation at Pat's church had an amazing opportunity, which they were willing to embrace. A drop-in center for low-income women, which had been started by two nuns, had closed, but the nuns were willing to turn over a neatly furnished center to whomever might feel called to keep it open.

Mary Claire, the volunteer clarinetist in the church, talked with me about her vision for the center. She imagined it providing counseling, addictions treatment, job training, spiritual formation, and a safe place for women to help each other. This was her generative dream, but there were no funds to make it happen. She had already formed a board to reopen the center, and the church was ready to help her by sheltering these fledgling efforts and accepting donations for the center, but they had no other resources but themselves.

Mary Claire had worked as the provincial educator for an Episcopal diocese. When her mother died, leaving Mary Claire and her siblings with two summer cottages in Maine, she risked her future, took early retirement, and moved to the smaller cottage, hoping she could find some kind of work by the end of the summer. She patched together three jobs to get by, but discovered that the house was simply too cold to live in year-round. So she spent all the money she had to buy a winterized house, and she took a job with the state doing home education for parents of kids in trouble. It was challenging and draining work, but it fed Mary Claire's desire to share her resources of education and experience as others worked to find the financial resources to keep the drop-in center open.

A year after my visit, I got an exultant e-mail from Mary Claire. The center now had enough funding to stay open, and she would be the full-time director. The nuns planted a seed in that community. Mary Claire's vision for keeping the center open was quietly contagious. The well-dressed women who brought soup for the opening have continued to build a network of volunteers. The church has continued to support her efforts, and Mary Claire is now finding new contacts for her interest in promoting home care for the dying—something she had experienced with her mother's death.

⟐

Living into an uncertain future takes courage and hopefulness. Both are chosen behaviors encouraged by a spiritual practice and a spiritual community. Each person that I spoke with during interviews for this book had discovered a spiritual practice to sustain their individual sense of call and had found others with whom they could share that call in order to give it form and shape. Sometimes that community structure came with a long history, like the Episcopal Church for Pat. Sometimes a new form arose out of a felt need, like the Wednesday Weeders for Jill or the center volunteers for Mary Claire. These kinds of intentional communities help us commit ourselves to holding a larger purpose, a wider vision for the world we live in.

We all need regular reminders that life itself is a gift and that death is not the end of the story. I find that sense of community at Seekers Church, where my weekly mission group gives me a place to reflect on my life and look for the growing edge where God is at work, changing me. Our weekly worship, regular classes, and silent retreats together provide a time of communal listening for deeper currents than I get from daily reflections with prayer, dreams, and journaling.

Others find companions in art classes, study groups, or work groups such as Habitat for Humanity, Bread for the World, or a local food bank. Public service is another venue for relating. Wherever you are lucky enough to find a few others who are also conscious of aging as a blessing instead of a curse, you can develop a community of practice that will help keep you sane and hopeful when all the evidence that our culture publicizes seems to point toward disaster and disintegration.

When human beings are willing to take their creative energies seriously, make connections with others who can help, and share their resources, change comes and healing happens. Relating is the key. Each of us has a unique gift, which is a combination of who we are and what we have lived through, and we need to find a place where that gift of our true selves can be received. Some people like to work alone but need those who can make connections. Others have gifts for creating organization but need someone else to provide vision and purpose. A call that takes root in the soul is always meant to be shared. At the core of this third round of call, beyond the confines of career and success, lies a field of spiritual connection waiting for each one of us.

Spiritual Practice: Intentional Community

Spiritual practice in community does not have to be complicated. If you are gathering with people who have a common intention, consider what your group might do to remind each other that your lives matter, that you are standing on the holy ground of call. That might include the simple act of forming a circle, lighting a candle, invoking the spirit of the group for the purpose of being together, and holding the space for whatever is to occur. Sometimes that means sitting in silence, listening for the whisper of God. Sometimes it means something more formal, more celebratory or liturgical. Relating to others in a community of spiritual practice will help you remember that you belong to something larger than yourself, that your life has meaning and purpose in the greater story of creation.

Questions to Ponder

1. Think of a time when a community (not necessarily your workplace) helped you do something that you had always wanted to do. Recall some of the important elements of that help. Do you have such a community now? If not, where might you find one?

2. Pick out a group of people (such as Wednesday Weeders) to create a change in your world that you want to see. How are you related to that group? How might you ask them to help with a change?

3. When you read the newspaper or listen to the news, is there some situation or group of people that tugs at your heart? Is there some specific action (such as the drop-in center) that they need? Is there some community that you might gather to meet that need?

EPILOGUE
Living Wholeheartedly

I do not feel betrayed or bereft ...
I am carrying my bit of being free of agenda—
... backpacking into the hereafter.

—M. C. Richards

Postcareer generativity is never guaranteed. Our fears of being old or irrelevant feed stasis and stagnation. They may cause us to grab for certainties, pay for security, and drive ourselves harder to stave off change. Our egos want control, want to be in charge, to guarantee fairness and reward for hard work—knowing all the while that, in the end, we cannot succeed at this. We can either befriend our aging bodies or die trying.

The rhythm of night and day is a reminder that creative aging is always shadowed by the threat of lassitude, boredom, decrepitude, depression, or drink, which may dog the end of a career and suppress the life-giving energies coursing through us. But the drama of every sunset is also a reminder that, as long as we are alive, the spiral of call never stops.

At this encore stage of life, we can revisit the first round of call and claim a new identity with wholeheartedness, trusting the full range of who we are—temperament, needs, experiences, abilities, and disabilities. We can take up the second round of call and find new opportunities to create work that can become a vocation simply by the presence we bring to it. We can embrace the third round of call and discover that we ourselves are the gift we've been waiting for. We can bring the unique gift of who we are and what we've lived through to whatever work we are here to do.

Although habits of the heart are hard to break, it is possible to awake from a long sleep and find ourselves renewed by hearing the call from our own soul's aliveness. It's never too late to listen and respond.

Surprisingly, it is the reality of death that makes our choices meaningful. It is the reality of sorrow that makes joy precious; the presence of evil makes love and generosity an everyday miracle. We can live out our span of days as unconscious as clams, or we can choose to claim the powerful gift of awareness. We can decide to wake up, to find meaning in discovering who we are and how we are connected to others on the same journey.

To be generative rather than despairing about the aging process requires that we see our lives from a longer perspective, as part of a greater story that will last beyond our particular time and place. Creative aging is a choice. We can either spend our lives in regret, bemoaning what we have apparently lost, or we can focus on the generative round of call that is unfolding in us. If we do the inner work of release and resistance, reclaiming and revelation, we can cross over into the outer expression of risk and relating. If we remember that transition always begins with endings, moves on to a wilderness period of testing and trying, and only then reaches the beginning of something new, then we can embrace this encore period of life with hope and curiosity, remembering always that it is our true nature to be creative, to be always birthing new ways of sharing our planet together.

As I approach my seventieth birthday, I'm deep into the third round of call. I'm heading homeward—not back to Bellingham, Washington, where I grew up, but "backpacking into the hereafter," as potter and painter M. C. Richards wrote to her friends just before she died. I'm conscious of what I've left behind as I move forward, stripped down to the bare essentials, through the rocky inward terrain of aging, just partially aware of what I've packed for the journey. This doesn't feel like a heroic journey, but it does feel deeply human, walking at a good clip, breathing deeply, eyes wide open.

If, as we cross the threshold into this gift of extra time that we have received so gratuitously, we can let our ego boundaries soften to a permeable state and let ourselves receive the grace that surrounds us every day, then we will find enough light to take the next step on the backpacker's trail that is ours on this journey of creative aging.

Suggestions for
Further Reading

Arrien, Angeles. *The Second Half of Life: Opening the Eight Gates of Wisdom.* Boulder, CO: Sounds True, 2007.

Bankson, Marjory Zoet. *The Soulwork of Clay: A Hands-On Approach to Spirituality.* Woodstock, VT: SkyLight Paths, 2008.

Bateson, Mary Catherine. *Composing a Life.* New York: Atlantic Monthly Press, 1989.

Bridges, William. *Transitions: Making Sense of Life's Changes.* Cambridge, MA: Da Capo Press, 2004.

Chittister, Joan. *The Gift of Years: Growing Older Gracefully.* New York: BlueBridge, 2008.

Eliot, T. S. *The Complete Poems and Plays, 1909–1950.* New York: Harcourt, Brace, 1952.

Freedman, Marc. *Encore: Finding Work That Matters in the Second Half of Life.* New York: PublicAffairs, 2007.

Fritz, Robert. *The Path of Least Resistance: Learning to Become the Creative Force in Your Own Life.* New York: Fawcett Columbine, 1989.

Hollis, James. *Finding Meaning in the Second Half of Life: How to Finally, Really Grow Up.* New York: Gotham Books, 2005.

———. *What Matters Most: Living a More Considered Life.* New York: Gotham Books, 2009.

Jung, C. G. *Memories, Dreams, Reflections.* New York: Vintage Books, 1965.

Kushner, Harold S. *When All You've Ever Wanted Isn't Enough.* New York: Summit Books, 1986.

Lawrence-Lightfoot, Sara. *The Third Chapter: Passion, Risk, and Adventure in the 25 Years After 50.* New York: Farrar, Straus & Giroux, 2009.

McMakin, Jacqueline. *Working from the Heart.* With Sonya Dyer. Washington, D.C.: Potter's House Bookservice, 1993.

Palmer, Parker J. *A Hidden Wholeness: The Journey toward an Undivided Life.* San Francisco: Jossey-Bass, 2004.

——. *Let Your Life Speak: Listening for the Voice of Vocation.* San Francisco: Jossey-Bass, 2000.

Raines, Robert. *A Time to Live: Seven Tasks of Creative Aging.* New York: Dutton Books, 1997.

Richards, M. C. *Centering in Pottery, Poetry, and the Person.* Middletown, CT: Wesleyan University Press, 1989.

Richmond, Lewis. *Work as a Spiritual Practice.* New York: Broadway Books, 1999.

Ryan, Thomas. *Soul Fire: Accessing Your Creativity.* Woodstock, VT: SkyLight Paths, 2008.

Scherer, John J. *Five Questions That Change Everything: Life Lessons at Work.* Fort Collins, CO: Word Keepers, 2009.

Schuster, John P. *Answering Your Call: A Guide for Living Your Deepest Purpose.* San Francisco: Berrett-Koehler, 2003.

Srode, Molly. *Creating a Spiritual Retirement: A Guide to the Unseen Possibilities in Our Lives.* Woodstock, VT: SkyLight Paths, 2003.

Srode, Molly, and Bernie. *Keeping Spiritual Balance as We Grow Older: More than 65 Creative Ways to Use Purpose, Prayer, and the Power of Spirit to Build a Meaningful Retirement.* Woodstock, VT: SkyLight Paths, 2004.

Taylor, Barbara Brown. *An Altar in the World: A Geography of Faith.* New York: HarperCollins, 2009.

Whitcomb, Holly W. *Seven Spiritual Gifts of Waiting.* Minneapolis: Augsburg Books, 2005.

Winton-Henry, Cynthia. *Dance—The Sacred Art: The Joy of Movement as a Spiritual Practice.* Woodstock, VT: SkyLight Paths, 2009.

——. *What the Body Wants.* With Phil Porter. Kelowna, BC: Northstone, 2004.

Woodman, Marion, and Elinor Dickson. *Dancing in the Flames: The Dark Goddess in the Transformation of Consciousness.* Boston: Shambhala, 1997.

Zander, Rosamund Stone, and Benjamin Zander. *The Art of Possibility: Transforming Personal and Professional Life.* New York: Penguin, 2000.

Inspiration

Restoring Life's Missing Pieces
The Spiritual Power of Remembering & Reuniting with People, Places, Things & Self
by Caren Goldman
A powerful and thought-provoking look at reunions of all kinds as roads to remembering and re-membering ourselves.
6 x 9, 208 pp, Quality PB, 978-1-59473-295-9 **$16.99**

How Did I Get to Be 70 When I'm 35 Inside?
Spiritual Surprises of Later Life
by Linda Douty
Encourages you to focus on the inner changes of aging to help you greet your later years as the grand adventure they can be.
6 x 9, 208 pp, Quality PB, 978-1-59473-297-3 **$16.99**

Spiritually Healthy Divorce: Navigating Disruption with Insight & Hope
by Carolyne Call
A spiritual map to help you move through the twists and turns of divorce.
6 x 9, 224 pp, Quality PB, 978-1-59473-288-1 **$16.99**

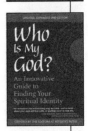

Who Is My God? 2nd Edition
An Innovative Guide to Finding Your Spiritual Identity
by the Editors at SkyLight Paths
Provides the Spiritual Identity Self-Test™ to uncover the components of your unique spirituality.
6 x 9, 160 pp, Quality PB, 978-1-59473-014-6 **$15.99**

God the What?
What Our Metaphors for God Reveal about Our Beliefs in God
by Carolyn Jane Bohler
Inspires you to consider a wide range of images of God in order to refine how you imagine God.
6 x 9, 192 pp, Quality PB, 978-1-59473-251-5 **$16.99**

Journeys of Simplicity
Traveling Light with Thomas Merton, Bashō,
Edward Abbey, Annie Dillard & Others
by Philip Harnden
Invites you to consider a more graceful way of traveling through life.
PB includes journal pages to help you get started on
your own spiritual journey.
5 x 7¼, 144 pp, Quality PB, 978-1-59473-181-5 **$12.99**
5 x 7¼, 128 pp, HC, 978-1-893361-76-8 **$16.95**

Or phone, fax, mail or e-mail to: SKYLIGHT PATHS Publishing
Sunset Farm Offices, Route 4 • P.O. Box 237 • Woodstock, Vermont 05091
Tel: (802) 457-4000 • Fax: (802) 457-4004 • www.skylightpaths.com
Credit card orders: (800) 962-4544 (8:30AM–5:30PM ET Monday–Friday)
Generous discounts on quantity orders. SATISFACTION GUARANTEED. Prices subject to change.

Judaism / Christianity / Islam / Interfaith

Christians & Jews—Faith to Faith: Tragic History, Promising Present, Fragile Future *by Rabbi James Rudin*
A probing examination of Christian-Jewish relations that looks at the major issues facing both faith communities. 6 x 9, 288 pp, HC, 978-1-58023-432-0 **$24.99***

Getting to the Heart of Interfaith
The Eye-Opening, Hope-Filled Friendship of a Pastor, a Rabbi and a Sheikh
by Pastor Don Mackenzie, Rabbi Ted Falcon and Imam Jamal Rahman
Offers many insights and encouragements for individuals and groups who want to tap into the promise of interfaith dialogue. 6 x 9, 192 pp, Quality PB, 978-1-59473-263-8 **$16.99**

Hearing the Call across Traditions: Readings on Faith and Service
Edited by Adam Davis; Foreword by Eboo Patel
Explores the connections between faith, service and social justice through the prose, verse and sacred texts of the world's great faith traditions.
6 x 9, 352 pp, Quality PB, 978-1-59473-303-1 **$18.99**; HC, 978-1-59473-264-5 **$29.99**

How to Do Good & Avoid Evil: A Global Ethic from the Sources of Judaism
by Hans Küng and Rabbi Walter Homolka; Translated by Rev. Dr. John Bowden
6 x 9, 224 pp, HC, 978-1-59473-255-3 **$19.99**

Blessed Relief: What Christians Can Learn from Buddhists about Suffering
by Gordon Peerman 6 x 9, 208 pp, Quality PB, 978-1-59473-252-2 **$16.99**

The Changing Christian World: A Brief Introduction for Jews
by Rabbi Leonard A. Schoolman 5½ x 8½, 176 pp, Quality PB, 978-1-58023-344-6 **$16.99***

Christians & Jews in Dialogue: Learning in the Presence of the Other *by Mary C. Boys and Sara S. Lee; Foreword by Dorothy C. Bass* 6 x 9, 240 pp, Quality PB, 978-1-59473-254-6 **$18.99**

Disaster Spiritual Care: Practical Clergy Responses to Community, Regional and National Tragedy Edited by Rabbi Stephen B. Roberts, BCJC, and Rev. Willard W.C. Ashley, Sr., DMin, DH
6 x 9, 384 pp, HC, 978-1-59473-240-9 **$40.00**

InterActive Faith: The Essential Interreligious Community-Building Handbook
Edited by Rev. Bud Heckman with Rori Picker Neiss; Foreword by Rev. Dirk Ficca
6 x 9, 304 pp, Quality PB, 978-1-59473-273-7 **$16.99**; HC, 978-1-59473-237-9 **$29.99**

The Jewish Approach to God: A Brief Introduction for Christians
by Rabbi Neil Gillman, PhD 5½ x 8½, 192 pp, Quality PB, 978-1-58023-190-9 **$16.95***

The Jewish Approach to Repairing the World (*Tikkun Olam*): A Brief Introduction for Christians *by Rabbi Elliot N. Dorff, PhD, with Rev. Cory Willson*
5½ x 8½, 256 pp, Quality PB, 978-1-58023-349-1 **$16.99***

The Jewish Connection to Israel, the Promised Land: A Brief Introduction for Christians *by Rabbi Eugene Korn, PhD* 5½ x 8½, 192 pp, Quality PB, 978-1-58023-318-7 **$14.99***

Jewish Holidays: A Brief Introduction for Christians *by Rabbi Kerry M. Olitzky and Rabbi Daniel Judson* 5½ x 8½, 176 pp, Quality PB, 978-1-58023-302-6 **$16.99***

Jewish Ritual: A Brief Introduction for Christians
by Rabbi Kerry M. Olitzky and Rabbi Daniel Judson 5½ x 8½, 144 pp, Quality PB, 978-1-58023-210-4 **$14.99***

Jewish Spirituality: A Brief Introduction for Christians *by Rabbi Lawrence Kushner*
5½ x 8½, 112 pp, Quality PB, 978-1-58023-150-3 **$12.95***

A Jewish Understanding of the New Testament *by Rabbi Samuel Sandmel;
New preface by Rabbi David Sandmel* 5½ x 8½, 368 pp, Quality PB, 978-1-59473-048-1 **$19.99***

Modern Jews Engage the New Testament: Enhancing Jewish Well-Being in a Christian Environment *by Rabbi Michael J. Cook, PhD* 6 x 9, 416 pp, HC, 978-1-58023-313-2 **$29.99***

Talking about God: Exploring the Meaning of Religious Life with Kierkegaard, Buber, Tillich and Heschel *by Daniel F. Polish, PhD* 6 x 9, 160 pp, Quality PB, 978-1-59473-272-0 **$16.99**

We Jews and Jesus: Exploring Theological Differences for Mutual Understanding
by Rabbi Samuel Sandmel; New preface by Rabbi David Sandmel
6 x 9, 192 pp, Quality PB, 978-1-59473-208-9 **$16.99**

Who Are the *Real* Chosen People? The Meaning of Chosenness in Judaism, Christianity and Islam *by Reuven Firestone, PhD*
6 x 9, 176 pp, Quality PB, 978-1-59473-290-4 **$16.99**; HC, 978-1-59473-248-5 **$21.99**

* A book from Jewish Lights, SkyLight Paths' sister imprint

Spiritual Poetry—The Mystic Poets

Experience these mystic poets as you never have before. Each beautiful, compact book includes a brief introduction to the poet's time and place, a summary of the major themes of the poet's mysticism and religious tradition, essential selections from the poet's most important works, and an appreciative preface by a contemporary spiritual writer.

Hafiz
The Mystic Poets
Preface by Ibrahim Gamard

Hafiz is known throughout the world as Persia's greatest poet, with sales of his poems in Iran today only surpassed by those of the Qur'an itself. His probing and joyful verse speaks to people from all backgrounds who long to taste and feel divine love and experience harmony with all living things.
5 x 7¼, 144 pp, HC, 978-1-59473-009-2 **$16.99**

Hopkins
The Mystic Poets
Preface by Rev. Thomas Ryan, CSP

Gerard Manley Hopkins, Christian mystical poet, is beloved for his use of fresh language and startling metaphors to describe the world around him. Although his verse is lovely, beneath the surface lies a searching soul, wrestling with and yearning for God.
5 x 7¼, 112 pp, HC, 978-1-59473-010-8 **$16.99**

Tagore
The Mystic Poets
Preface by Swami Adiswarananda

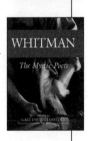

Rabindranath Tagore is often considered the Shakespeare of modern India. A great mystic, Tagore was the teacher of W. B. Yeats and Robert Frost, the close friend of Albert Einstein and Mahatma Gandhi, and the winner of the Nobel Prize for Literature. This beautiful sampling of Tagore's two most important works, *The Gardener* and *Gitanjali,* offers a glimpse into his spiritual vision that has inspired people around the world.
5 x 7¼, 144 pp, HC, 978-1-59473-008-5 **$16.99**

Whitman
The Mystic Poets
Preface by Gary David Comstock

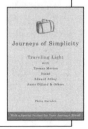

Walt Whitman was the most innovative and influential poet of the nineteenth century. This beautiful sampling of Whitman's most important poetry from *Leaves of Grass,* and selections from his prose writings, offers a glimpse into the spiritual side of his most radical themes—love for country, love for others and love of Self.
5 x 7¼, 192 pp, HC, 978-1-59473-041-2 **$16.99**

Journeys of Simplicity
Traveling Light with Thomas Merton, Bashō, Edward Abbey, Annie Dillard & Others
by Philip Harnden

Invites you to consider a more graceful way of traveling through life.
PB includes journal pages to help you get started on your own spiritual journey.
5 x 7¼, 144 pp, Quality PB, 978-1-59473-181-5 **$12.99**
5 x 7¼, 128 pp, HC, 978-1-893361-76-8 **$16.95**

Children's Spiritual Biography

Ten Amazing People
And How They Changed the World
by Maura D. Shaw; Foreword by Dr. Robert Coles
Full-color illus. by Stephen Marchesi

For ages 7 & up

Black Elk • Dorothy Day • Malcolm X • Mahatma Gandhi • Martin Luther King, Jr. • Mother Teresa • Janusz Korczak • Desmond Tutu • Thich Nhat Hanh • Albert Schweitzer

Shows kids that spiritual people can have an exciting impact on the world around them. Kids will delight in reading about these amazing people and what they accomplished through their words and actions.

8½ x 11, 48 pp, Full-color illus., HC, 978-1-893361-47-8 **$17.95**
For ages 7 & up

Spiritual Biographies for Young People—For Ages 7 & Up

By Maura D. Shaw; Illus. by Stephen Marchesi
6¾ x 8¼, 32 pp, Full-color and b/w illus., Hardcover

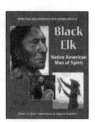 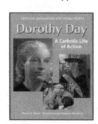 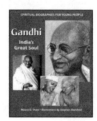 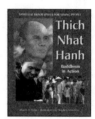

Black Elk: Native American Man of Spirit
Through historically accurate illustrations and photos, inspiring age-appropriate activities and Black Elk's own words, this colorful biography introduces children to a remarkable person who ensured that the traditions and beliefs of his people would not be forgotten.
978-1-59473-043-6 **$12.99**

Dorothy Day: A Catholic Life of Action
Introduces children to one of the most inspiring women of the twentieth century, a down-to-earth spiritual leader who saw the presence of God in every person she met. Includes practical activities, a timeline and a list of important words to know.
978-1-59473-011-5 **$12.99**

Gandhi: India's Great Soul
The only biography of Gandhi that balances a simple text with illustrations, photos and activities that encourage children and adults to talk about how to make changes happen without violence. Introduces children to important concepts of freedom, equality and justice among people of all backgrounds and religions.
978-1-893361-91-1 **$12.95**

Thich Nhat Hanh: Buddhism in Action
Warm illustrations, photos, age-appropriate activities and Thich Nhat Hanh's own poems introduce a great man to children in a way they can understand and enjoy. Includes a list of important Buddhist words to know.
978-1-893361-87-4 **$12.95**

Children's Spirituality

Adam & Eve's First Sunset: God's New Day
by Sandy Eisenberg Sasso; Full-color illus. by Joani Keller Rothenberg 9 x 12, 32 pp, Full-color illus., HC,
978-1-58023-177-0 **$17.95** *For ages 4 & up (A book from Jewish Lights, SkyLight Paths' sister imprint)*

Because Nothing Looks Like God
by Lawrence Kushner and Karen Kushner; Full-color illus. by Dawn W. Majewski
Invites parents and children to explore the questions we all have about God.
11 x 8½, 32 pp, Full-color illus., HC, 978-1-58023-092-6 **$17.99**
For ages 4 & up (A book from Jewish Lights, SkyLight Paths' sister imprint)
Also available: **Teacher's Guide,** 8½ x 11, 22 pp, PB, 978-1-58023-140-4 **$6.95** *For ages 5–8*

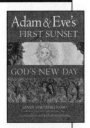

But God Remembered: Stories of Women from Creation to the
Promised Land *by Sandy Eisenberg Sasso; Full-color illus. by Bethanne Andersen*
A fascinating collection of four different stories of women only briefly mentioned in biblical tradition and religious texts.
9 x 12, 32 pp, Full-color illus., Quality PB, 978-1-58023-372-9 **$8.99**; HC, 978-1-879045-43-9 **$16.95**
For ages 8 & up (A book from Jewish Lights, SkyLight Paths' sister imprint)

Cain & Abel: Finding the Fruits of Peace
by Sandy Eisenberg Sasso; Full-color illus. by Joani Keller Rothenberg
A sensitive recasting of the ancient tale shows we have the power to deal with anger
in positive ways. "Editor's Choice" —American Library Association's *Booklist*
9 x 12, 32 pp, Full-color illus., HC, 978-1-58023-123-7 **$16.95** *For ages 5 & up (A book from
Jewish Lights, SkyLight Paths' sister imprint)*

Does God Hear My Prayer?
by August Gold; Full-color photos by Diane Hardy Waller
Introduces preschoolers and young readers to prayer and how it helps them
express their own emotions.
10 x 8½, 32 pp, Full-color photo illus., Quality PB, 978-1-59473-102-0 **$8.99** *For ages 3–6*

The 11th Commandment: Wisdom from Our Children *by The Children of America*
"If there were an Eleventh Commandment, what would it be?" Children of many
religious denominations across America answer this question—in their own drawings and words. "A rare book of spiritual celebration for all people, of all ages,
for all time." —*Bookviews* 8 x 10, 48 pp, Full-color illus., HC, 978-1-879045-46-0 **$16.95**
For all ages (A book from Jewish Lights, SkyLight Paths' sister imprint)

For Heaven's Sake *by Sandy Eisenberg Sasso; Full-color illus. by Kathryn Kunz Finney*
Heaven is often found where you least expect it. 9 x 12, 32 pp, Full-color illus., HC,
978-1-58023-054-4 **$16.95** *For ages 4 & up (A book from Jewish Lights, SkyLight Paths' sister imprint)*

God in Between *by Sandy Eisenberg Sasso; Full-color illus. by Sally Sweetland*
A magical, mythical tale that teaches that God can be found where we are.
9 x 12, 32 pp, Full-color illus., HC, 978-1-879045-86-6 **$16.95** *For ages 4 & up (A book from Jewish
Lights, SkyLight Paths' sister imprint)*

God's Paintbrush: Special 10th Anniversary Edition
Invites children of all faiths and backgrounds to encounter God through moments
in their own lives. 11 x 8½, 32 pp, Full-color illus., HC, 978-1-58023-195-4 **$17.95** *For ages 4 & up*
(A book from Jewish Lights, SkyLight Paths' sister imprint)
Also available: **God's Paintbrush Teacher's Guide** 8½ x 11, 32 pp, PB, 978-1-879045-57-6 **$8.95**
God's Paintbrush Celebration Kit: A Spiritual Activity Kit for Teachers and
Students of All Faiths, All Backgrounds 9½ x 12, 40 Full-color Activity Sheets & Teacher Folder
w/ complete instructions, HC, 978-1-58023-050-6 **$21.95**
Additional activity sheets available:
8-Student Activity Sheet Pack (40 sheets/5 sessions), 978-1-58023-058-2 **$19.95**
Single-Student Activity Sheet Pack (5 sessions), 978-1-58023-059-9 **$3.95**
Also available: **I Am God's Paintbrush** (A Board Book)
by Sandy Eisenberg Sasso; Full-color illus. by Annette Compton
5 x 5, 24 pp, Full-color illus., Board Book, 978-1-59473-265-2 **$7.99** *For ages 0–4*

Children's Spirituality—Board Books

Adam & Eve's New Day
by Sandy Eisenberg Sasso; Full-color illus. by Joani Keller Rothenberg
A lesson in hope for every child who has worried about what comes next.
Abridged from *Adam & Eve's First Sunset*.
5 x 5, 24 pp, Full-color illus., Board Book, 978-1-59473-205-8 **$7.99** For ages 0–4

How Did the Animals Help God?
by Nancy Sohn Swartz; Full-color illus. by Melanie Hall
Abridged from *In Our Image*, God asks all of nature to offer gifts to humankind—
with a promise that they will care for creation in return.
5 x 5, 24 pp, Full-color illus., Board Book, 978-1-59473-044-3 **$7.99** For ages 0–4

How Does God Make Things Happen?
by Lawrence and Karen Kushner; Full-color illus. by Dawn W. Majewski
A charming invitation for young children to explore how God makes things happen in
our world. Abridged from *Because Nothing Looks Like God*.
5 x 5, 24 pp, Full-color illus., Board Book, 978-1-893361-24-9 **$7.95** For ages 0–4

What Does God Look Like?
by Lawrence and Karen Kushner; Full-color illus. by Dawn W. Majewski
A simple way for young children to explore the ways that we "see" God. Abridged
from *Because Nothing Looks Like God*.
5 x 5, 24 pp, Full-color illus., Board Book, 978-1-893361-23-2 **$7.99** For ages 0–4

What Is God's Name?
by Sandy Eisenberg Sasso; Full-color illus. by Phoebe Stone
Everyone and everything in the world has a name. What is God's name? Abridged
from the award-winning *In God's Name*.
5 x 5, 24 pp, Full-color illus., Board Book, 978-1-893361-10-2 **$7.99** For ages 0–4

Where Is God? by Lawrence and Karen Kushner; Full-color illus. by
Dawn W. Majewski A gentle way for young children to explore how God is with
us every day, in every way. Abridged from *Because Nothing Looks Like God*.
5 x 5, 24 pp, Full-color illus., Board Book, 978-1-893361-17-1 **$7.99** For ages 0–4

What You Will See Inside ...

This important series of books, each with many full-color photos, is
designed to show children ages 6 and up the who, what, when,
where, why and how of traditional houses of worship, liturgical celebrations and rituals of different world faiths, empowering them to
respect and understand their own religious traditions—and those of
their friends and neighbors.

What You Will See Inside a Catholic Church
by Reverend Michael Keane; Foreword by Robert J. Kealey, EdD
Full-color photos by Aaron Pepis
8½ x 10½, 32 pp, Full-color photos, HC, 978-1-893361-54-6 **$17.95**

Also available in Spanish: **Lo que se puede ver dentro de una iglesia católica**
8½ x 10½, 32 pp, Full-color photos, HC, 978-1-893361-66-9 **$16.95**

What You Will See Inside a Hindu Temple
by Dr. Mahendra Jani and Dr. Vandana Jani; Full-color photos by Neirah Bhargava and Vijay Dave
8½ x 10½, 32 pp, Full-color photos, HC, 978-1-59473-116-7 **$17.99**

What You Will See Inside a Mosque
by Aisha Karen Khan; Full-color photos by Aaron Pepis
8½ x 10½, 32 pp, Full-color photos, Quality PB, 978-1-59473-257-7 **$8.99**

What You Will See Inside a Synagogue
by Rabbi Lawrence A. Hoffman, PhD, and Dr. Ron Wolfson; Full-color photos by Bill Aron
8½ x 10½, 32 pp, Full-color photos, Quality PB, 978-1-59473-256-0 **$8.99**

Children's Spirituality

Remembering My Grandparent: A Kid's Own Grief Workbook in the Christian Tradition *by Nechama Liss-Levinson, PhD, and Rev. Molly Phinney Baskette, MDiv* 8 x 10, 48 pp, 2-color text, HC, 978-1-59473-212-6 **$16.99** *For ages 7 & up*

Does God Ever Sleep? *by Joan Sauro, CSJ*
A charming nighttime reminder that God is always present in our lives.
10 x 8½, 32 pp, Full-color photos, Quality PB, 978-1-59473-110-5 **$8.99** *For ages 3–6*

Does God Forgive Me? *by August Gold; Full-color photos by Diane Hardy Waller*
Gently shows how God forgives all that we do if we are truly sorry.
10 x 8½, 32 pp, Full-color photos, Quality PB, 978-1-59473-142-6 **$8.99** *For ages 3–6*

God Said Amen *by Sandy Eisenberg Sasso; Full-color illus. by Avi Katz*
A warm and inspiring tale that shows us that we need only reach out to each other to find the answers to our prayers.
9 x 12, 32 pp, Full-color illus., HC, 978-1-58023-080-3 **$16.95**
For ages 4 & up (A book from Jewish Lights, SkyLight Paths' sister imprint)

How Does God Listen? *by Kay Lindahl; Full-color photos by Cynthia Maloney*
How do we know when God is listening to us? Children will find the answers to these questions as they engage their senses while the story unfolds, learning how God listens in the wind, waves, clouds, hot chocolate, perfume, our tears and our laughter.
10 x 8½, 32 pp, Full-color photos, Quality PB, 978-1-59473-084-9 **$8.99** *For ages 3–6*

In God's Hands *by Lawrence Kushner and Gary Schmidt; Full-color illus. by Matthew J. Baek*
9 x 12, 32 pp, Full-color illus., HC, 978-1-58023-224-1 **$16.99** *For ages 5 & up (A book from Jewish Lights, SkyLight Paths' sister imprint)*

In God's Name *by Sandy Eisenberg Sasso; Full-color illus. by Phoebe Stone*
Like an ancient myth in its poetic text and vibrant illustrations, this award-winning modern fable about the search for God's name celebrates the diversity and, at the same time, the unity of all the people of the world.
9 x 12, 32 pp, Full-color illus., HC, 978-1-879045-26-2 **$16.99**
For ages 4 & up (A book from Jewish Lights, SkyLight Paths' sister imprint)

Also available in Spanish: El nombre de Dios
9 x 12, 32 pp, Full-color illus., HC, 978-1-893361-63-8 **$16.95**

In Our Image: God's First Creatures
by Nancy Sohn Swartz; Full-color illus. by Melanie Hall
A playful new twist on the Genesis story—from the perspective of the animals. Celebrates the interconnectedness of nature and the harmony of all living things.
9 x 12, 32 pp, Full-color illus., HC, 978-1-879045-99-6 **$16.95**
For ages 4 & up (A book from Jewish Lights, SkyLight Paths' sister imprint)

Noah's Wife: The Story of Naamah
by Sandy Eisenberg Sasso; Full-color illus. by Bethanne Andersen
This new story, based on an ancient text, opens readers' religious imaginations to new ideas about the well-known story of the Flood. When God tells Noah to bring the animals of the world onto the ark, God also calls on Naamah, Noah's wife, to save each plant on Earth.
9 x 12, 32 pp, Full-color illus., HC, 978-1-58023-134-3 **$16.95**
For ages 4 & up (A book from Jewish Lights, SkyLight Paths' sister imprint)

Also available: Naamah: Noah's Wife (A Board Book)
by Sandy Eisenberg Sasso; Full-color illus. by Bethanne Andersen
5 x 5, 24 pp, Full-color illus., Board Book, 978-1-893361-56-0 **$7.99** *For ages 0–4*

Where Does God Live? *by August Gold and Matthew J. Perlman*
Helps children and their parents find God in the world around us with simple, practical examples children can relate to.
10 x 8½, 32 pp, Full-color photos, Quality PB, 978-1-893361-39-3 **$8.99** *For ages 3–6*

Prayer / Meditation

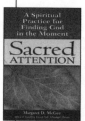

Sacred Attention: A Spiritual Practice for Finding God in the Moment
by Margaret D. McGee
Framed on the Christian liturgical year, this inspiring guide explores ways to develop a practice of attention as a means of talking—and listening—to God.
6 x 9, 144 pp, Quality PB, 978-1-59473-291-1 **$16.99**

Women of Color Pray: Voices of Strength, Faith, Healing, Hope and Courage
Edited and with Introductions by Christal M. Jackson
Through these prayers, poetry, lyrics, meditations and affirmations, you will share in the strong and undeniable connection women of color share with God.
5 x 7¼, 208 pp, Quality PB, 978-1-59473-077-1 **$15.99**

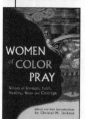

Secrets of Prayer: A Multifaith Guide to Creating Personal Prayer in Your Life   *by Nancy Corcoran, CSJ*
This compelling, multifaith guidebook offers you companionship and encouragement on the journey to a healthy prayer life. 6 x 9, 160 pp, Quality PB, 978-1-59473-215-7 **$16.99**

Prayers to an Evolutionary God
by William Cleary; Afterword by Diarmuid O'Murchu
Inspired by the spiritual and scientific teachings of Diarmuid O'Murchu and Teilhard de Chardin, reveals that religion and science can be combined to create an expanding view of the universe—an evolutionary faith.
6 x 9, 208 pp, HC, 978-1-59473-006-1 **$21.99**

The Art of Public Prayer, 2nd Edition: Not for Clergy Only
by Lawrence A. Hoffman, PhD 6 x 9, 288 pp, Quality PB, 978-1-893361-06-5 **$19.99**

A Heart of Stillness: A Complete Guide to Learning the Art of Meditation
by David A. Cooper 5½ x 8½, 272 pp, Quality PB, 978-1-893361-03-4 **$18.99**

Meditation without Gurus: A Guide to the Heart of Practice
by Clark Strand 5½ x 8½, 192 pp, Quality PB, 978-1-893361-93-5 **$16.95**

Praying with Our Hands: 21 Practices of Embodied Prayer from the World's Spiritual Traditions *by Jon M. Sweeney; Photos by Jennifer J. Wilson; Foreword by Mother Tessa Bielecki; Afterword by Taitetsu Unno, PhD*
8 x 8, 96 pp, 22 duotone photos, Quality PB, 978-1-893361-16-4 **$16.95**

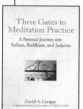

Three Gates to Meditation Practice: A Personal Journey into Sufism, Buddhism, and Judaism   *by David A. Cooper* 5½ x 8½, 240 pp, Quality PB, 978-1-893361-22-5 **$16.95**

Prayer / M. Basil Pennington, OCSO

Finding Grace at the Center, 3rd Edition: The Beginning of Centering Prayer   *with Thomas Keating, OCSO, and Thomas E. Clarke, SJ; Foreword by Rev. Cynthia Bourgeault, PhD* A practical guide to a simple and beautiful form of meditative prayer. 5 x 7¼, 128 pp, Quality PB, 978-1-59473-182-2 **$12.99**

The Monks of Mount Athos: A Western Monk's Extraordinary Spiritual Journey on Eastern Holy Ground   *Foreword by Archimandrite Dionysios*
Explores the landscape, monastic communities and food of Athos.
6 x 9, 352 pp, Quality PB, 978-1-893361-78-2 **$18.95**

Psalms: A Spiritual Commentary   *Illus. by Phillip Ratner*
Reflections on some of the most beloved passages from the Bible's most widely read book.   6 x 9, 176 pp, 24 full-page b/w illus., Quality PB, 978-1-59473-234-8 **$16.99**

The Song of Songs: A Spiritual Commentary   *Illus. by Phillip Ratner*
Explore the Bible's most challenging mystical text.
6 x 9, 160 pp, 14 full-page b/w illus., Quality PB, 978-1-59473-235-5 **$16.99**
HC, 978-1-59473-004-7 **$19.99**

Bible Stories / Folktales

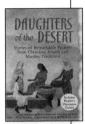

Abraham's Bind & Other Bible Tales of Trickery, Folly, Mercy and Love *by Michael J. Caduto*
New retellings of episodes in the lives of familiar biblical characters explore relevant life lessons. 6 x 9, 224 pp, HC, 978-1-59473-186-0 **$19.99**

Daughters of the Desert: Stories of Remarkable Women from Christian, Jewish and Muslim Traditions *by Claire Rudolf Murphy, Meghan Nuttall Sayres, Mary Cronk Farrell, Sarah Conover and Betsy Wharton*
Breathes new life into the old tales of our female ancestors in faith. Uses traditional scriptural passages as starting points, then with vivid detail fills in historical context and place. Chapters reveal the voices of Sarah, Hagar, Huldah, Esther, Salome, Mary Magdalene, Lydia, Khadija, Fatima and many more. Historical fiction ideal for readers of all ages.
5½ x 8½, 192 pp, Quality PB, 978-1-59473-106-8 **$14.99** Inc. reader's discussion guide
HC, 978-1-893361-72-0 **$19.95**

The Triumph of Eve & Other Subversive Bible Tales
by Matt Biers-Ariel
These engaging retellings of familiar Bible stories are witty, often hilarious and always profound. They invite you to grapple with questions and issues that are often hidden in the original texts.
5½ x 8½, 192 pp, Quality PB, 978-1-59473-176-1 **$14.99**

Also available: **The Triumph of Eve Teacher's Guide**
8½ x 11, 44 pp, PB, 978-1-59473-152-5 **$8.99**

Wisdom in the Telling
Finding Inspiration and Grace in Traditional Folktales and Myths Retold
by Lorraine Hartin-Gelardi
6 x 9, 192 pp, HC, 978-1-59473-185-3 **$19.99**

Religious Etiquette / Reference

How to Be a Perfect Stranger, 5th Edition: The Essential Religious Etiquette Handbook *Edited by Stuart M. Matlins and Arthur J. Magida*
The indispensable guidebook to help the well-meaning guest when visiting other people's religious ceremonies. A straightforward guide to the rituals and celebrations of the major religions and denominations in the United States and Canada from the perspective of an interested guest of any other faith, based on information obtained from authorities of each religion. Belongs in every living room, library and office. Covers:
African American Methodist Churches • Assemblies of God • Bahá'í Faith • Baptist • Buddhist • Christian Church (Disciples of Christ) • Christian Science (Church of Christ, Scientist) • Churches of Christ • Episcopalian and Anglican • Hindu • Islam • Jehovah's Witnesses • Jewish • Lutheran • Mennonite/Amish • Methodist • Mormon (Church of Jesus Christ of Latter-day Saints) • Native American/First Nations • Orthodox Churches • Pentecostal Church of God • Presbyterian • Quaker (Religious Society of Friends) • Reformed Church in America/Canada • Roman Catholic • Seventh-day Adventist • Sikh • Unitarian Universalist • United Church of Canada • United Church of Christ

"The things Miss Manners forgot to tell us about religion."
—*Los Angeles Times*

"Finally, for those inclined to undertake their own spiritual journeys … tells visitors what to expect." —*New York Times*

6 x 9, 432 pp, Quality PB, 978-1-59473-294-2 **$19.99**

The Perfect Stranger's Guide to Funerals and Grieving Practices: A Guide to Etiquette in Other People's Religious Ceremonies *Edited by Stuart M. Matlins*
6 x 9, 240 pp, Quality PB, 978-1-893361-20-1 **$16.95**

The Perfect Stranger's Guide to Wedding Ceremonies: A Guide to Etiquette in Other People's Religious Ceremonies *Edited by Stuart M. Matlins*
6 x 9, 208 pp, Quality PB, 978-1-893361-19-5 **$16.95**

Spiritual Practice

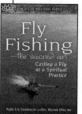

Fly Fishing—The Sacred Art: Casting a Fly as a Spiritual Practice
by Rabbi Eric Eisenkramer and Rev. Michael Attas, MD
Illuminates what fly fishing can teach you about reflection, awe and wonder; the benefits of solitude; the blessing of community and the search for the Divine.
5½ x 8½, 192 pp (est), Quality PB, 978-1-59473-299-7 **$16.99**

Lectio Divina—The Sacred Art: Transforming Words & Images into Heart-Centered Prayer *by Christine Valters Paintner, PhD*
Expands the practice of sacred reading beyond scriptural texts and makes it accessible in contemporary life. 5½ x 8½, 240 pp, Quality PB, 978-1-59473-300-0 **$16.99**

Haiku—The Sacred Art: A Spiritual Practice in Three Lines
by Margaret D. McGee 5½ x 8½, 192 pp, Quality PB, 978-1-59473-269-0 **$16.99**

Dance—The Sacred Art: The Joy of Movement as a Spiritual Practice
by Cynthia Winton-Henry 5½ x 8½, 224 pp, Quality PB, 978-1-59473-268-3 **$16.99**

Spiritual Adventures in the Snow: Skiing & Snowboarding as Renewal for Your Soul *by Dr. Marcia McFee and Rev. Karen Foster; Foreword by Paul Arthur*
5½ x 8½, 208 pp, Quality PB, 978-1-59473-270-6 **$16.99**

Divining the Body: Reclaim the Holiness of Your Physical Self *by Jan Phillips*
8 x 8, 256 pp, Quality PB, 978-1-59473-080-1 **$16.99**

Everyday Herbs in Spiritual Life: A Guide to Many Practices
by Michael J. Caduto; Foreword by Rosemary Gladstar
7 x 9, 208 pp, 20+ b/w illus., Quality PB, 978-1-59473-174-7 **$16.99**

Giving—The Sacred Art: Creating a Lifestyle of Generosity
by Lauren Tyler Wright 5½ x 8½, 208 pp, Quality PB, 978-1-59473-224-9 **$16.99**

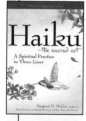

Hospitality—The Sacred Art: Discovering the Hidden Spiritual Power of Invitation and Welcome *by Rev. Nanette Sawyer; Foreword by Rev. Dirk Ficca*
5½ x 8½, 208 pp, Quality PB, 978-1-59473-228-7 **$16.99**

Labyrinths from the Outside In: Walking to Spiritual Insight—A Beginner's Guide
by Donna Schaper and Carole Ann Camp
6 x 9, 208 pp, b/w illus. and photos, Quality PB, 978-1-893361-18-8 **$16.95**

Practicing the Sacred Art of Listening: A Guide to Enrich Your Relationships and Kindle Your Spiritual Life *by Kay Lindahl* 8 x 8, 176 pp, Quality PB, 978-1-893361-85-0 **$16.95**

Recovery—The Sacred Art: The Twelve Steps as Spiritual Practice *by Rami Shapiro; Foreword by Joan Borysenko, PhD* 5½ x 8½, 240 pp, Quality PB, 978-1-59473-259-1 **$16.99**

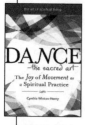

Running—The Sacred Art: Preparing to Practice *by Dr. Warren A. Kay; Foreword by Kristin Armstrong* 5½ x 8½, 160 pp, Quality PB, 978-1-59473-227-0 **$16.99**

The Sacred Art of Chant: Preparing to Practice
by Ana Hernández 5½ x 8½, 192 pp, Quality PB, 978-1-59473-036-8 **$15.99**

The Sacred Art of Fasting: Preparing to Practice
by Thomas Ryan, CSP 5½ x 8½, 192 pp, Quality PB, 978-1-59473-078-8 **$15.99**

The Sacred Art of Forgiveness: Forgiving Ourselves and Others through God's Grace
by Marcia Ford 8 x 8, 176 pp, Quality PB, 978-1-59473-175-4 **$18.99**

The Sacred Art of Listening: Forty Reflections for Cultivating a Spiritual Practice
by Kay Lindahl; Illus. by Amy Schnapper 8 x 8, 160 pp, b/w illus., Quality PB, 978-1-893361-44-7 **$16.99**

The Sacred Art of Lovingkindness: Preparing to Practice
by Rabbi Rami Shapiro; Foreword by Marcia Ford 5½ x 8¼, 176 pp, Quality PB, 978-1-59473-151-8 **$16.99**

Sacred Attention: A Spiritual Practice for Finding God in the Moment
by Margaret D. McGee 6 x 9, 144 pp, Quality PB, 978-1-59473-291-1 **$16.99**

Soul Fire: Accessing Your Creativity
by Thomas Ryan, CSP 6 x 9, 160 pp, Quality PB, 978-1-59473-243-0 **$16.99**

Thanking & Blessing—The Sacred Art: Spiritual Vitality through Gratefulness
by Jay Marshall, PhD; Foreword by Philip Gulley 5½ x 8½, 176 pp, Quality PB, 978-1-59473-231-7 **$16.99**

Spirituality & Crafts

Beading—The Creative Spirit: Finding Your Sacred Center through the Art of Beadwork *by Rev. Wendy Ellsworth*
Invites you on a spiritual pilgrimage into the kaleidoscope world of glass and color. 7 x 9, 240 pp, 8-page color insert, 40+ b/w photos and 40 diagrams, Quality PB, 978-1-59473-267-6 **$18.99**

Contemplative Crochet: A Hands-On Guide for Interlocking Faith and Craft *by Cindy Crandall-Frazier; Foreword by Linda Skolnik*
Illuminates the spiritual lessons you can learn through crocheting.
7 x 9, 208 pp, b/w photos, Quality PB, 978-1-59473-238-6 **$16.99**

The Knitting Way: A Guide to Spiritual Self-Discovery
by Linda Skolnik and Janice MacDaniels Examines how you can explore and strengthen your spiritual life through knitting.
7 x 9, 240 pp, b/w photos, Quality PB, 978-1-59473-079-5 **$16.99**

The Painting Path: Embodying Spiritual Discovery through Yoga, Brush and Color *by Linda Novick; Foreword by Richard Segalman*
Explores the divine connection you can experience through art.
7 x 9, 208 pp, 8-page color insert, plus b/w photos,
Quality PB, 978-1-59473-226-3 **$18.99**

The Quilting Path: A Guide to Spiritual Discovery through Fabric, Thread and Kabbalah *by Louise Silk*
Explores how to cultivate personal growth through quilt making.
7 x 9, 192 pp, b/w photos and illus., Quality PB, 978-1-59473-206-5 **$16.99**

The Scrapbooking Journey: A Hands-On Guide to Spiritual Discovery
by Cory Richardson-Lauve; Foreword by Stacy Julian Reveals how this craft can become a practice used to deepen and shape your life.
7 x 9, 176 pp, 8-page color insert, plus b/w photos, Quality PB, 978-1-59473-216-4 **$18.99**

The Soulwork of Clay: A Hands-On Approach to Spirituality
by Marjory Zoet Bankson; Photos by Peter Bankson
Takes you through the seven-step process of making clay into a pot, drawing parallels at each stage to the process of spiritual growth.
7 x 9, 192 pp, b/w photos, Quality PB, 978-1-59473-249-2 **$16.99**

Kabbalah / Enneagram
(Books from Jewish Lights Publishing, SkyLight Paths' sister imprint)

Cast in God's Image: Discover Your Personality Type Using the Enneagram and Kabbalah *by Rabbi Howard A. Addison, PhD* 7 x 9, 176 pp, Quality PB, 978-1-58023-124-4 **$16.95**

Ehyeh: A Kabbalah for Tomorrow *by Rabbi Arthur Green, PhD*
6 x 9, 224 pp, Quality PB, 978-1-58023-213-5 **$18.99**

The Enneagram and Kabbalah, 2nd Edition: Reading Your Soul
by Rabbi Howard A. Addison, PhD 6 x 9, 192 pp, Quality PB, 978-1-58023-229-6 **$16.99**

The Gift of Kabbalah: Discovering the Secrets of Heaven, Renewing Your Life on Earth
by Tamar Frankiel, PhD 6 x 9, 256 pp, Quality PB, 978-1-58023-141-1 **$16.95**

God in Your Body: Kabbalah, Mindfulness and Embodied Spiritual Practice
by Jay Michaelson 6 x 9, 272 pp, Quality PB, 978-1-58023-304-0 **$18.99**

Jewish Mysticism and the Spiritual Life: Classical Texts, Contemporary Reflections
Edited by Dr. Lawrence Fine, Dr. Eitan Fishbane and Rabbi Or N. Rose
6 x 9, 256 pp, HC, 978-1-58023-434-4 **$24.99**

Kabbalah: A Brief Introduction for Christians
by Tamar Frankiel, PhD 5½ x 8½, 208 pp, Quality PB, 978-1-58023-303-3 **$16.99**

Zohar: Annotated & Explained *Translation & Annotation by Daniel C. Matt;*
Foreword by Andrew Harvey 5½ x 8½, 176 pp, Quality PB, 978-1-893361-51-5 **$15.99**

Spirituality

The Heartbeat of God: Finding the Sacred in the Middle of Everything
by Katharine Jefferts Schori; Foreword by Joan Chittister, OSB
Explores our connections to other people, to other nations and with the environment through the lens of faith. 6 x 9, 240 pp, HC, 978-1-59473-292-8 **$21.99**

A Dangerous Dozen: Twelve Christians Who Threatened the Status Quo but Taught Us to Live Like Jesus
by the Rev. Canon C. K. Robertson, PhD; Foreword by Archbishop Desmond Tutu
Profiles twelve visionary men and women who challenged society and showed the world a different way of living. 6 x 9, 208 pp, Quality PB, 978-1-59473-298-0 **$16.99**

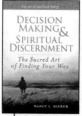

Decision Making & Spiritual Discernment: The Sacred Art of Finding Your Way *by Nancy L. Bieber*
Presents three essential aspects of Spirit-led decision making: willingness, attentiveness and responsiveness. 5½ x 8½, 208 pp, Quality PB, 978-1-59473-289-8 **$16.99**

Laugh Your Way to Grace: Reclaiming the Spiritual Power of Humor
by Rev. Susan Sparks A powerful, humorous case for laughter as a spiritual, healing path. 6 x 9, 176 pp, Quality PB, 978-1-59473-280-5 **$16.99**

Living into Hope: A Call to Spiritual Action for Such a Time as This
by Rev. Dr. Joan Brown Campbell; Foreword by Karen Armstrong
A visionary minister speaks out on the pressing issues that face us today, offering inspiration and challenge. 6 x 9, 208 pp, HC, 978-1-59473-283-6 **$21.99**

Claiming Earth as Common Ground: The Ecological Crisis through the Lens of Faith
by Andrea Cohen-Kiener; Foreword by Rev. Sally Bingham
6 x 9, 192 pp, Quality PB, 978-1-59473-261-4 **$16.99**

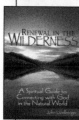

Bread, Body, Spirit: Finding the Sacred in Food
Edited and with Introductions by Alice Peck 6 x 9, 224 pp, Quality PB, 978-1-59473-242-3 **$19.99**

Creating a Spiritual Retirement: A Guide to the Unseen Possibilities in Our Lives
by Molly Srode 6 x 9, 208 pp, b/w photos, Quality PB, 978-1-59473-050-4 **$14.99**

Creative Aging: Rethinking Retirement and Non-Retirement in a Changing World
by Marjory Zoet Bankson 6 x 9, 160 pp, Quality PB, 978-1-59473-281-2 **$16.99**

Keeping Spiritual Balance as We Grow Older: More than 65 Creative Ways to Use Purpose, Prayer, and the Power of Spirit to Build a Meaningful Retirement
by Molly and Bernie Srode 8 x 8, 224 pp, Quality PB, 978-1-59473-042-9 **$16.99**

Hearing the Call across Traditions: Readings on Faith and Service
Edited by Adam Davis; Foreword by Eboo Patel
6 x 9, 352 pp, Quality PB, 978-1-59473-303-1 **$18.99**; HC, 978-1-59473-264-5 **$29.99**

Honoring Motherhood: Prayers, Ceremonies & Blessings
Edited and with Introductions by Lynn L. Caruso 5 x 7¼, 272 pp, HC, 978-1-59473-239-3 **$19.99**

Journeys of Simplicity: Traveling Light with Thomas Merton, Bashō, Edward Abbey, Annie Dillard & Others *by Philip Harnden*
5 x 7¼, 144 pp, Quality PB, 978-1-59473-181-5 **$12.99**; 128 pp, HC, 978-1-893361-76-8 **$16.95**

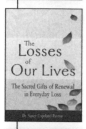

The Losses of Our Lives: The Sacred Gifts of Renewal in Everyday Loss
by Dr. Nancy Copeland-Payton 6 x 9, 192 pp, HC, 978-1-59473-271-3 **$19.99**

Renewal in the Wilderness: A Spiritual Guide to Connecting with God in the Natural World *by John Lionberger*
6 x 9, 176 pp, b/w photos, Quality PB, 978-1-59473-219-5 **$16.99**

Soul Fire: Accessing Your Creativity
by Thomas Ryan, CSP 6 x 9, 160 pp, Quality PB, 978-1-59473-243-0 **$16.99**

A Spirituality for Brokenness: Discovering Your Deepest Self in Difficult Times
by Terry Taylor 6 x 9, 176 pp, Quality PB, 978-1-59473-229-4 **$16.99**

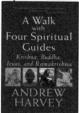

A Walk with Four Spiritual Guides: Krishna, Buddha, Jesus, and Ramakrishna
by Andrew Harvey 5½ x 8½, 192 pp, b/w photos & illus., Quality PB, 978-1-59473-138-9 **$15.99**

The Workplace and Spirituality: New Perspectives on Research and Practice
Edited by Dr. Joan Marques, Dr. Satinder Dhiman and Dr. Richard King
6 x 9, 256 pp, HC, 978-1-59473-260-7 **$29.99**

Women's Interest

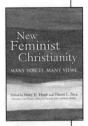

About SKYLIGHT PATHS Publishing

SkyLight Paths Publishing is creating a place where people of different spiritual traditions come together for challenge and inspiration, a place where we can help each other understand the mystery that lies at the heart of our existence.

Through spirituality, our religious beliefs are increasingly becoming a part of our lives—rather than *apart* from our lives. While many of us may be more interested than ever in spiritual growth, we may be less firmly planted in traditional religion. Yet, we do want to deepen our relationship to the sacred, to learn from our own as well as from other faith traditions, and to practice in new ways.

SkyLight Paths sees both believers and seekers as a community that increasingly transcends traditional boundaries of religion and denomination—people wanting to learn from each other, *walking together, finding the way.*

For your information and convenience, at the back of this book we have provided a list of other SkyLight Paths books you might find interesting and useful. They cover the following subjects:

Buddhism / Zen	Global Spiritual	Monasticism
Catholicism	Perspectives	Mysticism
Children's Books	Gnosticism	Poetry
Christianity	Hinduism /	Prayer
Comparative	Vedanta	Religious Etiquette
Religion	Inspiration	Retirement
Current Events	Islam / Sufism	Spiritual Biography
Earth-Based	Judaism	Spiritual Direction
Spirituality	Kabbalah	Spirituality
Enneagram	Meditation	Women's Interest
	Midrash Fiction	Worship